D1197478

POLITICAL PARTICIPATION

115212

POLITICAL PARTICIPATION

How and Why Do People Get Involved in Politics?

LESTER W. MILBRATH
State University of New York at Buffalo

329
—
M6 38

Rand McNally College Publishing Company/Chicago

Alverno College
Library Media Center
Milwaukee, Wisconsin

Rand McNally Political Science Series

Morton Grodzins, *Late Advisory Editor*

Current printing (last digit)
15 14 13 12 11 10 9 8 7

Copyright © 1965 by Rand McNally College Publishing Company
All rights reserved
Printed in U.S.A.
Library of Congress Catalog Card Number: 65:18592

To

My Mother and Father

PREFACE

The perception that a book like this was needed grew out of my experience in teaching a section on political participation in courses on public opinion, voting behavior, and political behavior. Although there is a considerable accumulation of research findings that one can bring to the attention of students working on this subject, they are scattered in a variety of books and articles. Furthermore, it is not possible to assign enough of these scattered materials to show students how research findings on political participation accumulate and thoroughly verify many propositions.

It seemed that the most clear and efficient way to present these findings was in the form of an inventory of propositions. The Political Science Department at Northwestern University has launched propositional inventories in several areas of substantive concern in the discipline and has experimented with several methods of abstracting and retrieving information from professional literature. This book is the product of one of those efforts. Detailing the evolution of our methods for abstraction and retrieval would take us far afield. However, I would like to thank my graduate seminar in political behavior (Fall, 1962) for their assistance in abstracting a large portion of the relevant literature. Reference to the Bibliography will indicate the magnitude of the task.

The propositions turned up by this search required organization into a theoretical framework if their full meaning was to be communicated; this I have tried to supply in the first chapter. Hopefully, I have succeeded well enough so that this book may be readily comprehended by college students at all levels. Even though the freshman can understand it, the graduate student, too, may find it a handy summary and reference. My class in public opinion and voting behavior, which is largely composed of sophomores, juniors, and seniors, is the audience I had in mind as I wrote.

Although most of the findings reported in the book are drawn from published literature, some original research is also reported. As a participant in a seminar on electoral research, sponsored by the Social Science Research Council and held at the Survey Research Center, University of Michigan, I was given access to data from the 1956 Presidential election study conducted by the Survey Research Center. Most of the tables in the book are drawn from these data. I am indebted to the Survey Research Center and to the Social Science Research Council for this opportunity.

I am especially grateful to Stein Rokkan and John Wahlke, both of whom counseled with me at the planning stages of the book and were good enough to review and criticize the first draft of the manuscript. Faculty and student participants in the Political Behavior Program at Northwestern also reviewed various sections of the manuscript as part of the continuing seminar held by that program; my colleagues Lee Anderson, Kenneth Janda, and David Minar gave me special help with certain sections. Michael Durkee assisted me during the planning stages and abstracted some materials. Two graduate seminars in political behavior and three undergraduate classes in public opinion and voting behavior have read the manuscript and given me the benefit of their puzzled queries and suggestions for changes. Jane Taylor was patient enough to type two drafts of the manuscript and caught many a grammatical slip in the process. Brent Rutherford suggested a superior version of Figure 4 in Chapter I. Lucia Boyden of the Rand McNally editorial staff has advised me at several stages of writing and production. The book could only benefit from all this help, and I am profoundly grateful. Finally, I would like to offer condolences to my wife, Kirsten, and my children, Linda Beate and Erik John, who had to suffer through many a boring hour while I pounded away at the typewriter.

L.W.M.

Evanston, Ill.
February, 1965

CONTENTS

INTRODUCTION

POLITICS COULD BE defined very broadly as the adjustment efforts of humans attempting to coexist in an interdependent relationship. This would mean that every form of human society would have some form of politics, and in a certain sense this is true. We recognize this when we talk about politics in private associations such as churches, businesses, pressure groups, social clubs, and so forth. Although it is undoubtedly valid to say that politics enters into the governance of private groups, such a broad definition dulls rather than sharpens our analysis. When "politics" becomes ubiquitous or universal, it begins to lose its meaning. We need a definition that will distinguish political from nonpolitical behavior.

This distinction can most readily be made in the context of defining a political system. We shall adopt Dahl's definition: "A political system is any persistent pattern of human relationships that involves, to a significant extent, power, rule, or authority" (1963, p. 6). In everyday life, we think of a political system as including not only formal government but also the pattern of human relationships that affect the decisions of that government. Thus, a political system includes certain organizations like political parties and pressure groups and also behaviors directed toward governmental decisions such as discussions about governmental policies and voting. Political behavior, then, is behavior which affects or is intended to affect the decisional outcomes of government. The politics of nongovernmental organizations are excluded from this definition. Behavior which affects the decisional outcomes of a church or a corporation, for example, even if it were typically political in form and content, would not be considered political behavior by this definition. Politics now can be defined as the process by which decisions about governmental outcomes are made.

Even by this narrower definition, it is fair to say that every human life is touched by politics. As the world becomes ever more populated and crowded, requiring human relationships to become ever more complex and interdependent, the impact of politics on human lives will become increasingly determinative. The adequacy of functioning of a political system may well be decisive for the happiness and well-being of the members of that society. Since the manner in which citizens participate in their political process is integral to the manner in which the system functions, the question of how and why persons become involved in politics is germane to the concerns of every man, as well as to the curious probings of social scientists.

People relate to their political system in a variety of ways. Some persons take the system for granted and are concerned only to adjust their behavior to its demands; others want to improve or transform it. Some have only a passive relationship to the system, while others are very actively involved. To some, the system is frightening and confusing; to others, it is an object to be explored and conquered. Some focus their attention on what the system demands from them, while others focus on the benefits they derive from the system.

Social scientists now have a sizable body of evidence that helps to explain differences in the ways persons relate the system. This book is an attempt to summarize the state of our knowledge about political participation. A summary, to be really serviceable, must integrate discrete facts into a somewhat comprehensive whole; thus, some sort of theory is required. Two initial steps toward such a theory are taken in the book. An inductive approach has been adopted: findings are examined and then sorted into propositions which, at least in some cases, form "islands of theory." Secondly, while the author has not attempted to build a grand over-all theory, he has set forth in Chapter I a model or sketch which suggests a way in which the variables associated with political participation may be related to one another. This sketch provides a common basis for thinking about political participation and also serves as a plan for presenting the empirical findings to follow. This model was not arrived at deductively from a set of assumptions and then imposed upon the data; rather, it was built up inductively from careful examination of the findings.

Although some attention is given to the functioning of the political system, the major concern of the book is to explain individual human behavior as it relates to the political system. Therefore, the human organism, rather than groups or the political system, usually is taken as the unit of analysis. Political system and political culture are important influences on individual political behavior, and we naturally expect differences in political behavior patterns from culture to culture (see Almond & Verba, 1963). At the same time, most social scientists assume that, at a basic level, human beings follow the same behavioral laws no matter what kind of culture they live in. We shall seek such behavioral laws holding across cultures as the analysis proceeds.

The available research evidence on political participation is not as complete as we would like to achieve. The greatest amount of evidence is about the political behavior of Americans. Most of the other data comes from western Europe, leaving only scatterings from the rest of the world. Furthermore, most of the evidence has been gathered in the last thirty years. These limitations require the caution that the generalizations set forth in the book may only apply in Western democracies in the mid-twentieth century. We can speculate that the generalizations will hold in other cultures and at other times, but certainty will have to await much more comprehensive investigation.

This book is primarily addressed to college students of political science, although research scholars and general readers may also find it interesting. It has deliberately been kept short so that it can be used as supplementary reading in college courses. The book presents an overview and synthesis of the findings on political participation, and concentration on this objective means that other considerations must be slighted. Exhaustive evaluations of methods and of the quality of evidence are not possible in the text. Rather than report the findings of any given study in full detail and in a single location in the text, findings are brought in to support points in the natural progression of discussion. Since studies are cited many times, only author and date of publication are given in the text and footnotes, but full citations can be found in the bibliography. The book is not a bibliographic essay on political participation, and the author makes no pretense that every relevant citation is given for each proposition. He has attempted, however, to be comprehensive in reporting empirically supported propositions about political participation. In the text, propositions are distinguished by level of confidence. Those in italics are propositions for which there is some evidence, but of which the author is not as confident as he is of those propositions in bold-face type. In the latter case, there is generally more than one study in support of the proposition.

I

CONCEPTUAL PROBLEMS OF POLITICAL PARTICIPATION

THE FIRST TASK is to find a way to think about political participation. Participation must be defined; variables relating to it must be specified; and the subject must be bounded so that it is kept to manageable size. A model to facilitate thinking about participation is sketched later in the chapter.

Clarity in social science research is facilitated by specifying a level of analysis. The distinction is usually made between macro and micro levels. In social science, the macro level refers to large social units such as a nation, or political system, or organization. The micro level refers to individuals and their behavior. "Micro" and "macro" are comparative rather than absolute terms, however, and in other sciences may have a different specific meaning. In biology, for example, "macro" means unusually large and "micro" means unusually small.

Although the emphasis in this book is on micro political behavior, some attention is given to macro characteristics as well. The behavior of the two systems is often interrelated; individual (micro) political behavior affects the behavior of the larger political system (macro); macro characteristics, in turn, affect micro behavior. The level of inquiry adopted by the analyst is determined partially by the kinds of questions he wishes to ask. The question, "How does a system of political parties affect the stability of a political regime?" requires a macro level of analysis. The major question for this book, "How and why do people get involved in politics?" requires emphasis on the micro level. Certain questions require a bridging of the two levels. Two such questions for this book are: "How do the characteristics of the political system affect the manner and extent of citizen participation in politics?" and "How do the participation patterns of citizens affect the functioning of the political system?"

DECISIONS ABOUT PARTICIPATION

Taking any political action generally requires two decisions: one must decide to act or not to act; and one must also decide the direction of his action. For example, a person not only decides to vote or not to vote, but also decides whom to vote for. Usually, the decision to perform an action like voting precedes the decision about the direction of the action, but the time sequence could be reversed. Sometimes, a person decides that he likes a candidate or a party before he makes up his mind to cast a vote. Certain actions do not involve a directional choice; for example, one cannot choose the government to which one wishes to pay taxes (without changing one's residence).

Decisions to act in a particular way often are accompanied by a third decision about the intensity, duration, and/or extremity of the action. Persons may lend political support mildly or vigorously, in a single instance or repeatedly. This third choice is intimately related to the other two. A person who takes vigorous and sustained political action very probably is strongly attracted in a certain direction. The very fact that he feels intensely makes it more likely that he will participate. This book focuses mainly on decisions to act or not to act and on decisions about the intensity and duration of the action.

Decisions about the direction of political action are properly another topic, and the book would be unduly expanded and complicated if an attempt were made to cover them here. Research findings about directional political choices are quite voluminous; furthermore, they are difficult to summarize, since the directions are specific as to setting and time. Generalizations applicable in one setting very likely are not applicable in other settings. For example, explanation of the factors leading some persons to prefer Eisenhower and others to prefer Stevenson in the 1956 presidential election in the United States[1] has little generalizability to the choice the voters made between candidates in the 1960 or 1964 presidential elections.

Settings have one thing in common, however—the concept of *status quo*. Persons can defend or try to change the *status quo*. Its defenders often are called conservatives, and those trying to change it often are called liberals. Liberal-conservative contention about what should be done with the *status quo* is a familiar theme through many centuries of political writing. Unfortunately, many directional choices cannot be fitted to this general liberal-conservative dimension; they are even more specific as to setting and time and, therefore, are even more difficult to summarize.

We have learned to be very cautious in generalizing about liberal-conservative directional choices. Although rational deliberation plays some role in a person's choosing a liberal or conservative direction, the rational aspect of such a choice should not be overemphasized. We shall see that relatively few people have sufficient information or sufficient understanding of the political system to be able to make a completely rational political choice. Furthermore, personality predispositions incline a person to screen out uncongenial stimuli from the mass that impinge on his sensory system. Research evidence suggests that at least some persons have personalities which are inclined either liberally or conservatively (McClosky, 1958; Milbrath, 1962). Presumably, persons inclined liberally or conservatively would adopt a corresponding position with respect to the *status quo* no matter what setting or era they lived in. For lack of empirical evidence, this assumption must remain purely speculative.

But one can ask, in turn, where liberal or conservative personalities come from. In part, a liberal or conservative inclination comes from environment: certain environments tend to produce liberals, and other environments tend to produce conservatives. It is a well-known generalization,

[1] For a very sophisticated analysis of these factors, see Campbell, et al. (1960).

for example, that lower-class environments tend to produce status-changers (liberals), and that upper-class environments tend to produce status-defenders (conservatives). But environment does not seem to account for all the variance in political personality; persons coming from very similar environments may have quite different personalities. This suggests that heredity also is a factor inclining some persons liberally and others conservatively. It is likely that there is a very complex interaction between heredity and environment which produces a personality inclined in a certain political direction. Social scientists, at this point, have only a very dim understanding of that interaction.

Many other factors can intervene between personality inclination and choice of political direction. Pressures from family or peer groups are very important. Predominant community beliefs tend to structure the way a person sees his political world. The presence of a certain configuration of information about a current political choice (in contrast to an alternative configuration of information) can strongly influence that choice.

The complex interaction of these multiple factors influencing direction of political choice produces decisions that may seem rather inconsistent to the political analyst. Studies of the American electorate show, for example, that a "liberal" position on foreign policy (internationalism in contrast to isolationism) is not related to a "liberal" position on domestic economic policy (welfare state in contrast to laissez faire). These two positions, in turn, seem to show no correlation with a "liberal" posture favoring integration in contrast to segregation (Campbell, et al., 1960). In the United States, the issue of the welfare state versus laissez faire most clearly and consistently distinguishes the Democratic (liberal) party from the Republican (conservative) party. It is only in this very limited way that the two American parties can be characterized as liberal or conservative. If the political setting should change, one could anticipate that labels about the political direction of a party might also change.

The point of this short digression concerning the factors involved in making choices about political direction is to suggest to the reader the complexity and magnitude of the problem of trying to explain such choices. It would take us too far afield to attempt a full explanation here. The reader need only be aware that a choice to take action nearly always requires a second choice about direction. Most of the findings to be discussed in this book are valid, no matter what directional choice the political actor makes.

THE ACTIVE-INACTIVE DIMENSION

Acting politically seems to have two types of contrasts: inactive and passive. Most citizens have both active and passive postures toward politics. Every person participates at least passively in the political system in which he lives. Mere compliance gives support to the existing regime and, therefore, is a type of political behavior.[2] There are other essentially passive responses to the political system: obeying laws, paying taxes, experiencing order and security. These passive behaviors are to be distinguished from the inactive counterparts to political action: nonvoting versus voting, noncontributing versus contributing, nonattending versus attending, and so forth.

Activity generally can be graded into quantities: some persons do more of a given thing than other persons. They may engage in an activity with greater frequency or regularity; they may give more hours or money at a time; they may participate in a wider repertoire of activities. Some persons are almost totally inactive; some are active in one type of behavior but passive in others; some are active in a wide variety of behaviors. Inactivity may be thought of as a zero or base point from which quantities of action can be measured.

Some additional characteristics of this general active-inactive dimension are discussed later in the chapter, but it might be helpful first to discuss several subdimensions of

[2]Almond & Verba (1963) have distinguished three roles: "participant," "subject," and "parochial." They have made the valuable point that each citizen plays all three roles at one time or another. "Participant" and "subject" roles (similar to the active-passive distinction made here) are both essential to a viable political regime. The "parochials" are similar to the inactives or those we later call the "apathetics."

political action. Certain of these subdimensional characteristics may make the prospect of taking an action attractive or unattractive to a potential participant. Learning theory tells us that if the costs of the action outweigh the anticipated rewards, the person is unlikely to perform the action.

Overt versus Covert

Some political actions are taken in full public view with exposure to the possibility of criticism and acclamation, while other actions are essentially private. A particular act, e.g., writing a letter, may be private in one context (a letter to a friend) and public in another (a letter to an editor). A discussion about politics with friends in a private home is quite different from a discussion of the same subject before the public media (such as a television discussion program). It is clear that in most cases the overt action has higher costs than the covert and thus requires higher rewards before persons engage in it.

Autonomous versus Compliant

All action is a response to a stimulus of some sort, but there is an important difference between a person who responds to an inner or general environmental stimulus (e.g., awareness that a campaign is in progress) and a person who responds to solicitation. Action taken in response to a request is certainly action rather than inaction, but it has passive overtones when compared to autonomous action. If the stimulus becomes virtually irresistible, such as a governmental order to pay taxes, action in compliance with the order may be seen as more passive than efforts to avoid compliance. It also is possible for a person to receive a request not to take an action; inaction, in this case, should be seen as compliance. Although the boundary between autonomy and compliance may be indistinct, there is an important difference in emphasis. Compliant behavior should, in most cases, be seen as the route of least cost or greatest reward.

Approaching versus Avoiding

Approaching behavior is characterized by a positive valence between actor and object, in contrast to avoiding behavior, characterized by a negative valence between actor and object. A valence is a relationship of either attraction or repulsion. If one likes ice cream, for example, he has a positive valence toward it. If one hates giving speeches, he has a negative valence toward the action. A valence is a property characterizing the actor and must have an object referent of which the actor is aware. The mere absence of action is not necessarily avoidance; the actor must withdraw or consciously abstain from an object or action before his behavior can be characterized as avoidance. For example, a person who does not make a political contribution because he is unaware that anyone wants him to contribute is not avoiding, but a person who does not contribute when he is requested to do so is. Avoiding behavior probably flows from anticipation of high costs, whereas approaching behavior probably follows the anticipation of high rewards.

Episodic versus Continuous

Some political action, such as voting, takes place only at specified times. The decision to take the action usually is conscious and often is preceded by a build-up period such as a campaign. Other actions, such as contacting a politician, holding an office, supporting a party, can be taken up at any time and for extended periods of time. Actions that can be continuous often become part of living patterns and may take on a routine character with little conscious decision to act or not to act. Continuous action generally has higher costs than episodic action, and a significant reward structure, preferably built in (like a salary), is needed to insure performance of the action. When measuring quantities or magnitudes of political action, it is important to note the episodic or continuous character of the action.

Inputs versus Outtakes

Certain behaviors constitute inputs to the political system (voting, campaigning, contacting officials, seeking office), in contrast to those which are outtakes or withdrawals from the system (services, public order, conflict resolution, justice). Scientists often speak of inputs and outputs when analyzing systems. Our concern here is to classify behavior of an individual with respect to a system; therefore, we speak of inputs and outtakes. This distinction can characterize the orientations or postures of individuals as well as characterize specific acts; some individuals emphasize outtakes in their orientation to the system and others emphasize inputs. It would be a little oversimple to classify inputs simply as costs and outtakes simply as rewards; many inputs carry auxiliary rewards (e.g., pleasure in voting), and many outtakes carry auxiliary costs (e.g., court costs in seeking justice).

Expressive versus Instrumental

Expressive political action focuses on symbol manipulation; mere engagement in the behavior is satisfying or drive-reducing. Instrumental action, in contrast, is oriented primarily toward manipulating and changing things. This subdimension of action is a motivational distinction, and the classification is made by looking at the situation and motivation of the actor. Consequently, it is difficult to classify specific acts as expressive or instrumental in every case. Casting a vote, for example, may be primarily expressive in one situation or for one person but primarily instrumental for another situation or person.

A person who behaves politically to satisfy expressive needs seems to consume the experience of engaging in the action. As his needs are satisfied by engaging in the action, his drive reduces, and the behavior ceases until a new need for expressive consumption arises. Participating in a demonstration, shouting a protest, engaging in political argument, pledging allegiance, are examples of specific acts that in most situations are expressive. The classification is one of motivation and emphasis; such acts also may have instrumental consequences.

Instrumental action typically follows through a long chain of events and intermediary goals leading to a final goal. Although participation in the action may be immediately satisfying to the actor, mere participation is not sufficient reward to produce the action; rather, reaching the goal is the source of drive reduction. Participating in a campaign, collecting information, volunteering for a job, are examples of acts that

are primarily instrumental in orientation
though their performance may provide
as well.[3]

Verbal versus Nonverbal

Most political acts require the use of v
some (talking about politics, writing letters
demand much more verbal ability than o....., (stuffing envelopes, marching in parades). A person who does not possess
verbal skills has a barrier to verbal participation; the cost of
participating in the activity may be so great that he avoids or
withdraws from verbal activities.

Social versus Nonsocial

This subdimension of action is closely related to the
verbal-nonverbal subdimension, but the two are not identical. Writing a letter or a speech, for example, is highly verbal
but does not require social interaction. Nearly all political
acts entail some minimal kind of social interaction, but it is
useful to distinguish the amount required. Soliciting political funds or campaigning from door to door, for example, requires much more social interaction than voting, attending a
meeting, joining a party, or making a monetary contribution.
The cost of participating in activities requiring a good deal
of social interaction is very high for persons who are not
skilled or at ease socially. Contrariwise, persons with a strong
need for social interaction may find sociable political activities very rewarding.

SUMMARIZING BEHAVIORAL DIMENSIONS

Unless the political analyst has thoroughly conceptual-
ized the dimensions of political action, his ability to think
about antecedent conditions for that action is limited. This
is especially important if one wants to be sure that he has
measured behavior in all its richness, or if one wishes to

[3] The most elaborate statement of expressive-instrumental orientation
to politics has been made by Himmelstrand (1960a; 1960b), but allusion to
a similar classification was made earlier by Riesman (1952).

FIGURE 1. Abstract Map of an Individual's Political Behavior.[a] The political acts shown in the various cells are illustrative for a hypothetical individual; for another individual, certain specific acts might appear in different cells.

		Inputs to the System by Individuals	Outtakes from the System by Individuals
Active	Instrumental	Leader selection (vote) Party activity Contributing money Keeping informed Volunteering Disobedience	Stewardship Communication opportunitie Services Economic opportunities Conflict resolution Justice
	Expressive	Allegiance Demonstrations Protests (vote) Political argument	National symbols Sense of identification Governmental protests Sense of superiority
Passive		Obedience Compliance Conscription Paying taxes Indifference	Public order Security

a
I am indebted to Professor David W. Minar, Northwestern University, for suggesting an earlier version of this figure.

measure all the relevant antecedent conditions. On the other hand, some means must be found for summarizing or classifying these dimensions to facilitate thinking about them. Classifications alert us to the ways that specific acts are similar or different and thus facilitate the search for variables that explain the occurrence of acts.

If one is concerned with only two or three dimensions of specific political acts, one possible way of summarizing these dimensions is shown in Figure 1, where the active-passive dimension is modified by the expressive-instrumental subdimension and by the input-outtake subdimension. The six-celled table or abstract map shown in Figure 1 suggests pigeonholes into which political behavior might be classified for certain analytical purposes. The acts shown in the various cells are illustrative for a given individual and are not analytically exclusive. The classification shown is from the perspective of the individual actor rather than of the

FIGURE 2. Illustrative Profile of a Political Contribution.

Active	Overt	Auton-omous	Approach-ing	Contin-uous	Outtake	Expres-sive	Verbal	Nonsocial
Inactive	Covert	Compliant	Avoiding	Episodic	Input	Instru-mental	Nonverbal	Social

political system. A given act (a vote, a protest, a contribution) may be primarily expressive in one setting or for a given individual but may be primarily instrumental in another setting or for another individual. Similarly, a specific act, such as making a contribution, may be primarily passive in one setting and primarily active in another.

A drawback of the type of map shown in Figure 1 is that it cannot be used for more than three, or possibly four, dimensions at one time. If one should try to draw a map that would categorize acts on nine dimensions at once, it would become so complicated and cumbersome as to lose all its utility. If, however, one can focus on a given act, he might turn to the profile method used by psychologists to summarize personality traits. A sample profile showing how a specific political act (making a monetary contribution to a party) might be sketched is shown in Figure 2. Although more information about a given political act is shown in such a profile than in the abstract map shown in Figure 1, the profile makes an assumption that is difficult to sustain. It assumes that the distance between the two extremes of a dimension can be measured and quantified, thereby enabling the assignment of a midpoint between them. In many cases, this assumption cannot be met. Certain dimensions (e.g., input-outtake) should more accurately be called categories, because there is no quantifiable distance between them. For other dimensions, political science has no reliable yardstick showing equal distance between units. Since the quantifiability assumption can be met only poorly or not at all for certain dimensions, such a profile may imply more precision than really exists.

The summarizing methods illustrated in Figures 1 and 2 have greater utility, at this point, for thinking about political behavior than for measuring it. They alert us to dimensions that may be overlooked in research. The reader will note as we report findings in subsequent chapters that most of these dimensions have been overlooked in research to date. In fact, a good deal of the research on political behavior has, so far, focused on a single active input: voting. Almost no attention has been given to outtakes. The discussion that follows focuses on the general active-inactive dimension (active inputs, to be more accurate) for two reasons: (1) it is a more general dimension than the subdimensions just discussed; (2) most research to date has asked simply whether a given active input occurred or not. A more elaborate dimensional framework would have no corresponding data to report.

THE GENERAL DIMENSION OF INVOLVEMENT

Political activity seems to have a patterning or clustering characteristic. This seems to be true in two senses: (1) variables that correlate with a specific political act tend to correlate with other political acts as well; (2) there seems to be a hierarchy of political involvement, in that persons at a given level of involvement tend to perform many of the same acts, including those performed by persons at lower levels of involvement. Each of these points is discussed in turn.

A broad generalization about political participation, which is widely supported in research findings, is that the same independent variables are related to a variety of political acts (Campbell, et al., 1960; Lane, 1959; Lazarsfeld, et al., 1944; Milbrath, 1960b; Milbrath & Klein, 1962; Pesonen, 1960; Pesonen, 1961; Rokkan, 1959; Rokkan & Campbell, 1960; Scheuch, 1961; Valen, 1961). For example, **higher socioeconomic status (SES) is positively associated with increased likelihood of participation in many different political acts; higher SES persons are more likely to vote, attend meetings,** join a party, campaign, and so forth.[4] There are some minor exceptions to the above generalization, but the repetitiveness with which a given independent variable correlates significantly with different political acts is impressive.

In addition to the above, research findings show that variables which are associated with political activity also are associated with nonpolitical community activity. Furthermore, **persons who are active in community affairs are much more likely than those not active to participate in politics.**[5] A comparative survey of five countries shows that in the United States and Great Britain, where levels of political participation are higher than in Germany, Italy, and Mexico, there is also a much higher level of social and organizational activity (Almond & Verba, 1963, ch. 10). This same study shows that participation in decisions in nonpolitical organizations is cumulative: persons participating in decisions in one organization are very likely to participate in decisions in other organizations as well. This pattern of behavior carries over to politics (p. 366). This evidence suggests that political participation can be thought of as a special case of general participation in social and community activities. Not everyone who is active socially is likely to become active in politics, but *it is probably easier for a person who enjoys social activity to enter politics than it is for a person who shuns social and community participation* (Milbrath, 1960b; Milbrath & Klein, 1962).

Political participation is often spoken of as being cumulative; persons who engage in one political action often engage in others as well. Figure 3 shows a hierarchical ranking of behaviors; with those most often engaged in at the bottom, and those least often engaged in at the top. The cumulative characteristic arises from the fact that persons who engage

[4] See Chapter V for a more complete discussion and citations of evidence.

[5] Agger & Goldrich (1958); Allardt (1962); Allardt, et al. (1958); Allardt & Pesonen (1960); Birch (1950); Buchanan (1956); Campbell (1962); Campbell & Kahn (1952); Coser (1951); Dahl (1961); Dogan (1961); Hastings (1954); Jensen (1960); Lane (1959); McClosky & Dahlgren (1959); Marvick & Nixon (1961); Milbrath & Klein (1962); Rokkan (1959); Rosenberg (1954-1955). Lipset (1960b, p. 67) has cited nine studies in five countries supporting this proposition.

FIGURE 3. Hierarchy of Political Involvement.

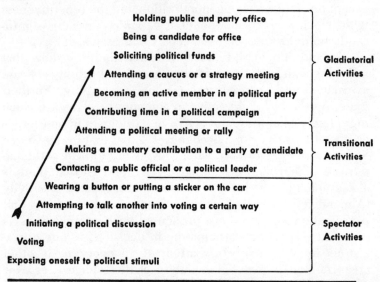

in the topmost behaviors are very likely to perform those lower in rank also. The hierarchy includes most, but not all, common political activities that characterize the normal process of a democracy. Although political demonstrations are considered a legitimate expression of political feeling in a democracy and are widely held, it is a behavior used by only certain sectors of society. Many other sectors look upon demonstrations as undignified and refuse to use them. Thus, this type of behavior does not fit into the hierarchy of political involvement in the United States. The hierarchy also does not apply to behavior designed to disrupt the normal operation of democratic political processes or to dislodge a regime from office by violent means; a general strike is an example of the former, and a palace revolt or *coup d'état* are examples of the latter.[6]

[6] In another sense, no political activity could be considered normal or routine for everyday existence. Persons turn to politics only when their basic physical needs, such as food, sex, sleep, safety, affection, have been met. The democratic processes listed in Figure 3 become normal, or even possible, only in societies where more basic needs are routinely satisfied. See Davies (1963), Chs. 1 and 2.

Another general characteristic of the levels of participation shown in Figure 3 is that they constitute a hierarchy of costs. Time and energy costs are least for the activities at the bottom of the hierarchy. Behaviors higher in the hierarchy obviously require a greater expenditure of energy and probably require a greater personal commitment. The particular ranking shown in the figure is based on percentages of Americans who engage in the behavior. Probably less than 1 per cent of the American adult population engage in the top two or three behaviors. Only about 4 or 5 per cent are active in a party, campaign, and attend meetings. About 10 per cent make monetary contributions, about 13 per cent contact public officials, and about 15 per cent display a button or sticker. Around 25 or 30 per cent try to proselyte others to vote a certain way, and from 40 to 70 per cent perceive political messages and vote in any given election.[7]

The ranking of a given item in the hierarchy may vary from election to election, from decade to decade, and from country to country. Since it is a hierarchy of costs, however, one would not expect the variation to be more than a shift of a rank or two. One must be cautious in comparing percentages of persons performing acts with the same name across political cultures. The political setting or context may put different content into the acts in the cultures being compared. For example, joining a political party seems to have a different social-psychological meaning in the United States than it does in Norway (Rokkan & Campbell, 1960. See the section on party membership later in this chapter). Provided the acts have similar psychological meaning in the cultures being compared, one could expect the ranking of the acts in the hierarchy to be similar.

The hierarchy seems to have a kind of internal logic, a natural progression of becoming involved in active politics. Although persons engaging in the topmost behaviors are likely also to engage in those behaviors ranking lower, the obverse does not hold. Minimally involved persons confine their actions to those acts ranking low in the hierarchy. As a person becomes more involved in politics, he engages

[7] Figures are drawn from Campbell, et al. (1960); Lane (1959); and Woodward & Roper (1950).

in a wider repertoire of political acts and moves upward in the hierarchy from the more frequent to the less frequent behaviors.

Although this implies a smooth progression from less to more participation, data on the American citizenry suggest that persons cluster into three general types or roles along the active-inactive dimension. One group participates only passively in the political process; they do not engage in any of the political acts shown in Figure 3. The second group is minimally involved in some or all of the first five activities shown in the hierarchy: seeking information, voting, discussing, proselyting, and displaying preference. A third, and quite small, group not only participates in the above activities but also is drawn into the political fray; they attend meetings, campaign, become active in a party, solicit money, run for and hold public and party office.

This division is reminiscent of the roles played at a Roman gladiatorial contest. A small band of gladiators battle fiercely to please the spectators, who have the power to decide their fate. The spectators in the stands cheer, transmit messages of advice and encouragement, and, at given periods, vote to decide who has won a particular battle (election). The apathetics do not bother to come to the stadium to watch the show. Taking a cue from the roles played in gladiatorial contests, the three political participation roles will be called "apathetics," "spectators," and "gladiators."

One of the striking things about these roles is their stability. From time to time, a gladiator who no longer enjoys the contest may withdraw to the role of spectator or even to apathetic. Occasionally, a spectator jumps into the political fray. But, by and large, personality and environmental factors encourage persons to stay in their roles. There seems to be a kind of threshold that must be crossed before a person changes role; this is especially characteristic of the transition from spectator to gladiator. A person needs an extra strong push from the environment (e.g., earnest solicitation from a friend) or needs to feel very strongly about an issue or a candidate before he will cross the threshold and become a political combatant.[8] Once the threshold is crossed and the new team member becomes integrated in his role, he usually participates in a wide repertoire of political acts.

Transitions between roles seem to occur at two points of the hierarchy shown in Figure 3. A person in transition from apathetic to spectator probably would seek information as a way of orienting himself as spectator and voter. Similarly, a person who chooses to lend more support than a cheer for his side in a political contest is likely to contact public officials, attend meetings, and make a monetary contribution as first transitional steps to becoming a full-fledged gladiator.

An additional role differentiation might be made within the gladiatorial category. Just as the political participation of spectators is nearly always in their leisure (nonwork) time, leisure-time participation characterizes a certain proportion of gladiators. Some gladiators, however, make politics their profession. In most settings, one should think of the professional politician as the most involved of all political roles.

About one-third of the American adult population can be characterized as politically apathetic or passive; in most cases, they are unaware, literally, of the political part of the world around them. Another 60 per cent play largely spectator roles in the political process; they watch, they cheer, they vote, but they do not do battle. In the purest sense of the word, probably only 1 or 2 per cent could be called gladiators. In order to have enough cases to analyze statistically, the definition of gladiator is expanded a bit in the following pages to include any person doing any of the acts in the top part of the hierarchy. Even by this expanded definition, the percentage of gladiators does not exceed 5 to 7. The proportions apply mainly to elections at which a President is chosen in the United States. The apathetic ranks probably are even larger

---

[8] Boynton & Bowman (1964) found in a study of recruitment to office in two cities that 26 per cent of local officials had been asked by someone else to become a candidate; another 24 per cent were strongly moved by some policy concern; only 25 per cent could be accounted for by general involvement and interest.

in strictly state and local elections; they are also larger in the American South. The five-nation study suggests that the apathetic ranks are also large in many other countries.[9]

CHARACTERISTICS OF SPECIFIC POLITICAL ACTS

Subsequent chapters focus on independent variables which explain, cause, or correlate with political participation as a broadly generalized dependent variable. It might be helpful, then, in this introductory chapter to discuss as concretely as possible the characteristics and dimensions of specific acts that go to make up the general dimension of active participation in politics. We shall follow the hierarchy of specific acts shown in Figure 3.

Exposure to Stimuli Perceived as Political

The person who hopes to deal effectively with his political environment must devote some energy to collecting information about it. This activity is elemental and fundamental to all other political activity, yet persons vary a good deal in the extent of their exposure to stimuli about politics. Despite the great flood of political stimuli available through the mass media, some persons are remarkably clever in exposing themselves to little or none of it. Variation in such exposure is a function of a person's predispositions and of the environment in which he lives. The senses of some persons are tuned to and pick up large amounts, whereas others seem to tune out all stimuli about politics. The environments of a few individuals are filled with political talk and political events (e.g., the son of a public office-holder) to the point where they could not avoid politics even if they tried. Other environments have so few stimuli about politics that an interested person has to seek them out deliberately. Generally, **the more political stimuli received by a person, the more likely he is to be active in politics.**

[9] They were especially large in Italy and Mexico, but Germany also had more apathetics than the United States and Great Britain. Almond & Verba (1963).

Voting

This most thoroughly researched of all political behaviors requires two decisions: first, the decision to engage in the act or not; and, second, the decision of which candidate or party to support. It is episodic in that it can occur only on days specified by law. These days are known well in advance, so that a person can gather relevant data and make a preliminary decision. Voting research also investigates the time of this decision and the frequency, regularity, and stability (in terms of direction) of the voting act.

Discussion and Opinion Leadership

Of all the stimuli about politics which a person may encounter, those which come through personal discussions are probably the most influential. Nearly everyone gets caught in a political discussion once in a while; some persons studiously avoid them, while others enjoy them and seek them out. Therefore, in thinking about discussions, it is important to distinguish initiator from recipient, leader from follower, missionary from unconvinced. A certain proportion of the population (about 20 per cent in the United States) regularly exercises political leadership in face-to-face interactions. These persons may be called opinion leaders. Opinion leadership may not be directed toward support of a party or candidate and, therefore, in many cases is a spectator rather than a gladiatorial activity. *Opinion leaders, however, are much more likely than followers to become gladiators.*

Wearing a Button or Putting a Sticker on the Car

Displaying one's partisan or candidate preference with a button or a sticker is another, but relatively weak, form of opinion leadership. Persons doing this often do not engage in additional proselyting activity to bring home their point. In many communities, it becomes a children's game to wear buttons displaying the candidate preference of their parents. The desire of children to conform to the button-wearing pattern and to have some preference to display instills party identification at an early age and helps make the adoption of partisan preference an accepted thing.

Petitioning Political Leaders

Only a relatively small proportion of citizens take the step of contacting political leaders and public officials.[10] This may be done by letter, telegram, telephone, or direct personal contact. A few persons, as a function of their position in the social and political structure, have normal daily interaction with political leaders and find it natural and useful to communicate their views to these men. This may constitute an easy transitional step to becoming a gladiator. Most persons, however, must take special pains to communicate with political leaders; seemingly, a large majority of them do not wish to take the trouble or may feel uncomfortable in attempting to do so. This barrier can be partially overcome by institutional intervention. A still larger proportion of citizens[11] belong to special-interest groups which represent them before government, often by hiring full-time lobbyists.

Making a Monetary Contribution

This act may be the first transitional step to becoming a gladiator, or it may be the extreme of spectator activity beyond which a citizen refuses to go. Like voting, it requires a decision to perform the act or not, and a second decision as to the direction of the act. Some busy and wealthy persons look upon monetary contributions as a substitute for their personal participation in gladiatorial activity. *Most contributions, however, come from gladiators themselves* (Heard, 1960; Milbrath, 1956a). They see political money as another weapon in their battle with the opposition. A few persons feel monetary contributions to politics are immoral, but this attitude is not widespread (Heard, 1960; Milbrath, 1956a).

Attending a Political Meeting

This is a spectator activity for some persons; they merely come to watch the show. No commitment of support is implied

---

[10]Woodward & Roper (1950) found 21 per cent in the United States.
[11]Woodward & Roper (1950) found 38 per cent in the United States.

by their presence. For others, however, attending meetings is a gladiatorial activity, and this is especially likely if they attend them more often than once or twice a year. Perhaps they are officials who have responsibility for organizing or participating in the meetings; perhaps they wish to show support of their party by helping to swell the turnout. Highly involved partisans also regularly attend caucuses and strategy meetings.

Campaigning

Political campaigns are episodic, but working in them can continue for several weeks. Some campaign work, like typing or stuffing envelopes, may be routine and boring. Most, however, requires considerable social interaction with other people, some of it in a pleading or salesman-like posture. This is especially true of canvassing from door to door or of making speeches. Evidence to be presented later shows that *self-confidence and a feeling of social ease are important prerequisites to participation in the socially interactive phase of campaigning.*

Active Party Membership

There are three ways in which a person could be said to be a party affiliate or member: (1) psychological identification with a party; (2) formal membership through payment of dues; and (3) active participation in party affairs. Psychological identification means that the person likes the party and is inclined to support it with a vote at election time. Identification can be ascertained by a survey question such as this: "Generally speaking, do you usually *think of yourself as* a Republican, a Democrat, an Independent, or what?"[12] A fairly large proportion of citizens identify with a political party (about 75 per cent in the United States). When a person says he thinks of himself as a Democrat or Republican, however, he very likely does not mean that he has a formal membership in the party.

Formal membership means that a person's name is en-

---

[12]This question, developed by Campbell, et al. (1954; 1960), has been used repeatedly in a variety of surveys. Emphasis has been added.

tered on the party rolls and that possibly he has been issued a membership card. Even this formal membership is loosely and variously defined. Some parties require only a declaration of support as a membership requirement; more commonly, dues or a monetary contribution are required.[13] In many instances, formal membership is not a commitment to activity on behalf of the party, and little is done to engage the "member" in party affairs. This is especially true of some European labor parties affiliated with labor unions and cooperative organizations. A formal institutional arrangement is worked out, whereby union members pay party dues along with their union dues and are blanketed into party membership unless they take the special trouble to "contract out." At the state and local level in the United States, there are party clubs to which citizens can belong and which constitute the effective working organizations of the parties. National parties, per se, have no provision for formal membership; a citizen can belong to a national party only through a state party.

The most meaningful kind of party membership (and the kind we are primarily concerned with in this book) is active party work. Party actives participate in meetings, caucuses, and conventions; they hold precinct, township, or ward office; they do the multitude of chores required around party or campaign headquarters; they canvass voters at election time; and so forth. Many party actives are leaders or aspire to be leaders, but, as in all organizations, there are also many followers. Active followers and leaders, taken together, constitute a relatively small cadre in most countries: usually less than 5 per cent of the citizenry are active party members.

Soliciting Political Funds

Relatively few persons have the position or the talent for soliciting money for parties or candidates. Some soliciting

[13] Kenneth Janda (1965) has studied the basis of affiliation of parties in all parts of the world. Of the 140 parties coded on this variable, 26 per cent have no formal membership requirement: a person merely needs to indicate support as in American parties. Half of the parties have an open requirement which grants membership to anyone who signs a form or pays dues. The remaining 24 per cent not only require a signature and dues but also require the potential member to go through a probationary period or have his application approved by party officials before membership is granted.

takes the form of door-to-door canvassing, usually for small contributions. Solicitors responsible for raising large sums of money not only need a talent for soliciting but also must be in a position (social, professional, commercial) that enables them to approach persons of wealth and prominence to request money. Any kind of soliciting requires social interaction, and a sociable personality trait is an important prerequisite to taking the action. Solicitors are important middlemen in politics who have ready access to official decision-makers and thus can transmit the desires of persons giving money (Heard, 1960, Ch. 10).

Office-Seeking and Holding

At the center of the political structure are the party and public office-holders. A special set of talents generally is required just to seek office. In certain party structures, where party discipline is strong and many jobs are filled by patronage, the main talent required for holding lesser office is the ability to carry out orders effectively. In other structures, or for holding higher office, it is important for a person to have strong initiative and great ego strength. These differences in talent requirements for different kinds of offices point up the analytical importance of distinguishing party and public office, appointive and elective office, lesser and higher office.

Protests and Demonstrations

Whether or not protest demonstrations are used seems to be affected more by political environment than most other political acts. They are, almost by definition, extraordinary rather than normal, and thus are difficult to place on Figure 3. Citizens with ready access to officials, and whose needs are routinely handled within the political system, tend to look upon demonstrations as undignified and not very effective. Persons in certain minorities who do not have ready access to decision-makers or who feel that the system does not respond to their demands have quite a different perspective on protest demonstrations. The very extraordinary character of the demonstrations helps get their message of dissatisfaction across to the public as well as to officials. Demonstrations also provide

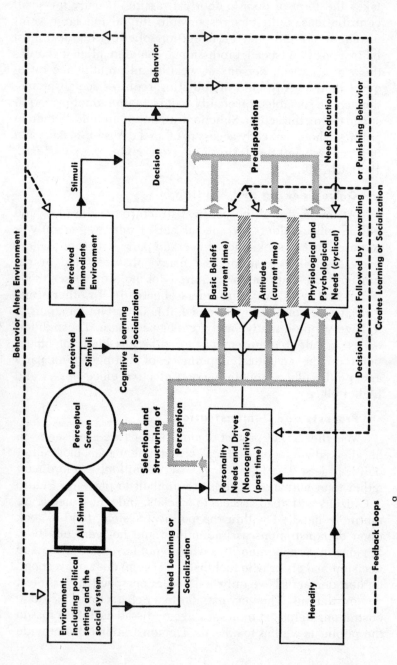

FIGURE 4. Model for Analysis of Individual Behavior.[a]

a
I am indebted to Brent Rutherford for helping draft the diagram.

an important expressive outlet for pent-up feelings of resentment and dissatisfaction. In other words, people who find demonstrations rewarding (usually deprived minorities) use them.

A CONCEPTUAL DIAGRAM OF POLITICAL BEHAVIOR VARIABLES

So far, we have been discussing ways of classifying and describing political behavior. Now we will try to think about its roots. We want to understand why people perform political acts and why they choose to perform some acts and not others. Description and explanation are not totally separate enterprises, but a shift to an emphasis on explanation leads to a search for relationships between variables that an emphasis on classification often does not.

Figure 4 shows a conceptual diagram that is useful for thinking about the causes of behavior. Designed to analyze behavior at the individual level, the model is largely based on concepts developed by learning theorists in psychology.[14] Although it is not irrelevant to the analysis of group or organizational behavior, more serviceable models could be developed for them. The diagram incorporates a time dimension. Those factors to the left of the diagram are presumed to have had their effect on behavior earlier in time than those factors to the right, which are presumed to precede behavior immediately. The explanation of the diagram is most parsimonious if we begin at the right and work back from decision and its immediate antecedents to factors that affect behavior at progressively earlier points in time.

Behavior is by definition continuous: there is no such thing as not behaving. Deciding to do nothing (make no change) or to sleep are still modes of behaving. An organism does not have the option of choosing not to choose. For analytical purposes, however, continuous behaving might be

---

[14] Two leading learning theorists have had the greatest impact on my own thinking about these matters: Clark L. Hull (1943) and Burrhus F. Skinner (1953). The discussion here merely borrows some of their concepts; it is not an exposition of their very complex and much more precise theories.

sliced into arbitrary units of time that can be called decisional units. The behaving organism constantly is choosing to do some one thing rather than another. The analysis of the factors that produce political behavior must begin with the immediate factors that produce a given decision.

The decision of an organism about its next act may be seen as a function of the interaction between the stimuli coming from the environment and the particular pattern of predispositions possessed by the organism at a given point in time. At any moment, several predispositions may be competing to take command of the organism, and several stimuli are available in the environment with the potentiality of interacting with those predispositions. The difficult task for the analyst of human behavior is to try to understand why a given set of stimuli and predispositions take precedence over several competing sets. Before speaking directly to that point, it is necessary to discuss the nature of predispositions and to introduce two concepts: a threshold concept and a selective perception concept.

Predispositions have been categorized analytically into three types in Figure 4: physiological and psychological needs, beliefs, and attitudes. This particular breakdown is most serviceable for explaining political behavior, but for other types of behavior, another classification might be more useful. The strength of a given predisposition is a function of the needs of the organism and of the amount of reinforcement that predisposition has received. Maslow (1943) has listed five main categories of human needs: (1) physical (food, water, sex, sleep, etc.); (2) safety (order, predictability of the environment); (3) love, affection, belongingness; (4) self-esteem; (5) self-actualization.[15] Some of these needs, especially the physical ones, rise and fall in strength cyclically. At times of great physical need, the organism becomes completely absorbed in filling that need. It is only when these needs can be satisfied somewhat routinely or readily that the organism can turn to social and political behavior. This tendency for physical needs to override all

---

[15]For a stimulating discussion of the way these needs affect political behavior, see Davies (1963), especially Chs. 1 and 2.

others when they are not satisfied is the main reason they are included as part of the predispositional complex in a diagram (Figure 4) which is primarily oriented toward analyzing social and political behavior.

The strength of more strictly political predispositions, such as beliefs and attitudes, is largely a function of a learning mechanism called reinforcement. If an individual performs a certain act and is rewarded for it, the predisposition to perform that act is reinforced. If the reward helps to satisfy a basic human need, such as that for food or affection, we say the predisposition has received a primary reinforcement; thus, rewards that satisfy basic human needs are known as primary reinforcers. If a certain stimulus is repeatedly present when primary reinforcement (reward) is received, the stimulus itself becomes rewarding; this is called secondary reinforcement. (The reader is reminded of Pavlov's classical experiment with a dog who heard a bell each time food was given him; eventually the dog salivated at the sound of the bell even though no food was present.) This principle of secondary reinforcement is very important, because many social behavior patterns are established by it. In addition, the concept helps us understand another very important mechanism, to be discussed shortly, called selective perception. If a certain behavior pattern has been reinforced again and again (the principle holds for both primary and secondary reinforcement), that behavior pattern, or predisposition, is said to have developed habit strength. The greater the habit strength, the greater the likelihood that that habit or predisposition will take command of the organism when several habits or predispositions are competing for command.

Figure 4 sets forth beliefs and attitudes as important political predispositions. Beliefs are defined as cognitions with an extra feeling of credibility which distinguishes them from cognitions which are not believed. I can cognize myself taking a trip in a spaceship to the moon, but I do not believe I will take such a trip. It is the *feeling* of credibility that makes a cognition believable; the cognition doesn't have to be true by some objective standard. People believe many things about which they have very poor information. Beliefs are expectancies and are close to what was called habit strength above. Attitudes are defined as feelings of like or dislike toward some object. A person may feel a duty to vote, or he may enjoy discussing politics, or he may feel an obligation to support his party with money or work. In these examples there is a positive valence between actor and object. There also can be a negative valence between them; a person may dislike door-to-door campaigning, he may be frightened of making speeches, he may dislike reading about politics.

Many cognitions are both beliefs and attitudes simultaneously. A person may believe very strongly that he is afraid to make a speech, that his party will win, or that it is his duty to vote. In fact, there is a tendency for persons to believe or expect those things they like or value. But it also is possible to have beliefs which are affectively neutral. One believes such things as "two plus two equals four," "there is an Africa," "steel is strong and hard," without necessarily having feelings of either like or dislike for them. Contrariwise, it is possible to like or dislike things one does not believe: "I would like to fly like a bird." Both beliefs and attitudes are included in the diagram because it is important to be aware that cognitions are affected by two kinds of feelings—credibility or incredibility and like or dislike. Another reason is that beliefs and cognitions have been relatively neglected in political behavior research, while there is already a good deal of research on attitudes. It is important to emphasize that political behavior is very dependent on the cognitions, and their credibility, that political actors hold about the political system in which they operate.

A threshold concept is helpful in understanding how predispositions compete to command the organism. The strength of a predisposition needed to take command of an organism is relative to the strength of the stimulus calling up the predisposition. Take, as an example, a person who has played mainly a spectator role in politics. None of the stimuli encountered in his daily environment have been strong enough to surmount his predispositional threshold and elicit active inputs to the system other than voting. The action of a personal friend in becoming a candidate for office, however, changes his personal environment. A request from his friend to help out in the campaign is sufficient to surmount his threshold and elicit new active political inputs. The stimulus which breaks the threshold is one which has previously received many primary reinforcements. The general predisposition to become active in politics has changed very little, but a particularly strong stimulus crosses the threshold. In this case, the stimulus not only acts upon the weak predisposition to become active in politics, but also activates a predisposition to help out a friend. A stimulus, then, need not be physically stronger or louder to activate a dormant behavior pattern (although the physical quality of the stimulus also is important); it may produce the relevant behavior by calling up additional predispositions until their combined force is sufficient to take command of the organism.

Returning to our example, suppose the man has some rewarding experiences while participating in his friend's campaign; he receives both primary and secondary reinforcement. The primary reinforcement strengthens his predisposition to campaign. The secondary reinforcement makes the stimuli associated with campaigning more attractive; they start to carry secondary rewards. The next time a political campaign starts up, a personal request may not be needed to elicit campaign behavior. The stimuli coming from the campaign will seem stronger to him, the strengthened predisposition to campaign will have lowered the stimulus threshold, and this is sufficient to get him to volunteer his services without a personal request.

The threshold concept is intimately related to a second concept we shall call the selective effect of predispositions upon perceptions. It is essential to the psychic economy of organisms that they perceive selectively. They have a perceptual screen which passes some stimuli and blocks others (see Figure 4). An organism would be overwhelmed if it attempted to attend to every stimulus impinging on its sensory organs. An organism may shift attention from one stimulus to another rather rapidly, but at any given instant the focus is upon relatively few.

How does the organism select the stimuli it will attend to? The answer to that is so difficult to study that psychologists speak of it as the "black box" which their methods cannot penetrate. Very generally, we can say that the choice of the stimulus seems to be a function both of the strength of the stimulus and of the strength of the predisposition with which that stimulus interacts. Very intense stimuli (loud sounds, bright lights, penetrating odors) are likely to get through the screen no matter how hard the individual tries to attend to something else. Also, stimuli that have been secondarily reinforced will be attractive and more likely to pass through the screen than those not so reinforced.

Stimuli also are screened for credibility. The judgment about credibility largely depends on how well the stimulus fits with the tightly woven pattern of cognitions already held as credible. Rokeach has told of hearing on a newscast one day that a camera had been invented that would take a picture of something that wasn't there; he rejected it as incredible. Later, he read that it took pictures of the heat remaining on a given spot after the object creating the heat had been moved. This fitted into his pattern of believed cognitions, and he could accept the new invention as credible.[16] Credibility is determined not only by fit with things already believed but also by what a person wishes to believe. It is a natural human failing to perceive selectively and to distort perception so that it bolsters cherished beliefs.

The stimulus attended to also depends on the state of the organism, so to speak. A strong predisposition will incline an organism to pick up stimuli relevant to that predisposition. This interaction can be illustrated by the example of the man campaigning for his friend. One evening after dinner, he is calling on voters door to door. As the evening progresses, his earlier satiation with food gives way to hunger. Stimuli associated with food, such as the smell of food or the sight of a restaurant sign, which earlier in the evening were ignored, now become relevant. The predisposition to eat interacts with the sight of a restaurant, and the man turns away from campaigning to eat a hamburger. With partial satia-

[16] Rokeach (1960), Part I, on the theory of belief systems, is very good.

tion, the predisposition to campaign once more takes command, until increasing fatigue inhibits the response. The organism must allow sleep to take over and replenish the predisposition for campaigning.

The way that an individual selectively attends to stimuli is in many ways analogous to the way a radio tuner functions. If the tuner responded at once to all the stimuli in its environment, it would produce an unintelligible garble. If the set is tuned to an appropriate frequency and the gain (volume control) is set sufficiently high, a usable response is emitted. Similarly, the human organism must be tuned to a stimulus (have a relevant predisposition), and the predisposition must be strong enough to lower the threshold so that the stimulus can cross it. The strength of the stimulus needed to activate a radio is relative to the gain setting (predisposition level); a strong stimulus activates the receiver at even a low gain setting, but a higher gain setting is needed for a weak signal. If the environmental stimulus ceases, the receiver ceases to respond. Similarly, the human organism cannot make a given response unless the appropriate stimulus calling it forth is available in the environment. If several stimuli are at about the same frequency (desirability), the stronger crowds out the weaker.

It was asked several pages back why a given set of stimuli and predispositions take precedence over several competing sets. With the threshold and selective perception concepts in mind, the answer should now be more intelligible. It is a function of the need of the organism, the stimuli available in the environment, and the strength of the various predispositions relevant to those stimuli. The organism responds only to stimuli that are present. It selects from those stimuli accordig to its needs and according to the strength of various competing predispositions, as these have been built up through numerous past reinforcemnts. Social science has not advanced sufficiently for us to be more precise at this time.

One can gain a bit more understanding, however, by asking where and how predispositions are developed? What are their roots? Figure 4 shows that beliefs and attitudes are a product of three factors: (1) personality needs and drives;

(2) cognitive learning (getting to know the world one lives in), and (3) learning which comes from behaving and then being rewarded or punished for that behavior. Physiological and psychological needs are developed partially from heredity and partially from personality needs and drives. The cyclical intensity of physiological needs is affected by the behavior of the organism in filling those needs; thus, a need-reduction arrow is drawn from behavior to that predispositional box.

Moving back a step in time, personality needs are a product of heredity, of need learning or socialization coming from the environment, and of rewards or punishments following from the various decisions of the organism. The reader will note that affective need learning has been conceptually distinguished from cognitive learning in the diagram; in real life, however, the two kinds of learning take place simultaneously.

Often, when explaining social and political behavior, we distinguish personality factors from environmental factors. (Such a distinction separates Chapter III from Chapters IV and V in this book.) According to such a distinction, personality would include all five of the following boxes on the diagram: heredity, personality needs and drives, physiological and psychological needs, beliefs, and attitudes.

Environmental impact on behavior is indirect, meaning that it is always mediated by personality. In past time, it has had its impact by forming the personality and belief system of the actor. Rewards and punishments, by which learning takes place, had come out of the environment. In addition, environment had produced nearly all the stimuli (the only exception being kinetic stimuli from inside the organism) for cognitive learning. In current time, environment provides the stimuli from which the individual selects his perceived environment; thus, current environment also is mediated by personality. Personality is not totally determinative, however, since it selects only from stimuli presented. Environmental stimuli not only incite action but also provide information about boundaries, barriers, norms, and costs which help the organism to choose among alternatives.

The behavior model presented in Figure 4 is dynamic.

The current behavior of an organism feeds back and has an impact on its future behavior (feedback loops are dotted lines on the diagram). Behavior alters the environment and thus changes the stimulus complex presented to the organism. In a discussion situation, for example, sending a message to one or more of the other actors usually stimulates a new message back to the first actor. An actor can move from one setting to another and thereby alter his stimulus complex. In a more long-range sense, lending or withholding political support partially determines whether a given set of officials win an election; this surely has an impact on environment. Behavior also can alter the organism's internal environment by satisfying a drive; when satiation occurs, the drive-fulfilling behavior ceases.

Another way that behavior feeds back and affects future behavior is through the learning mechanism. Nearly all decisions have rewarding or punishing consequences through which the organism learns habits, beliefs, attitudes, and drives. The complex mechanisms by which learning occurs are a central theoretical preoccupation of modern psychology, and a thorough description of them would be too elaborate for inclusion here. We can say, however, that an explanation of political behavior must include an examination of the stimuli present, of the impact of personality on selecting from those stimuli, and of the needs and predispositions competing for command of the organism. When we examine connections between environmental factors and political behavior, either we are indirectly measuring the impact of environment in shaping personality or we are seeing how the current environment presents opportunities and barriers to the actor. Finding the key to full understanding lies in our ability to unravel the complex learning process that mediates between the person and his environment.

The conceptual diagram sketched in Figure 4 does not have the predictive power expected of a full-fledged model. It does not, for example, enable us to predict which precise set of antecedent factors will produce one complex of predispositions and which set is needed to produce a differing complex. The major utility of the diagram is in locating and tentatively relating the variables that seem to determine behavior. The reader should keep the diagram in mind as he reads the subsequent chapters, because their organization is based on the categories of variables shown here. The variables have been given unequal research attention (scholars tend to do the easy things first), so the coverage is somewhat uneven.

We shall begin with the variables close to behavior in current time. Chapter II examines participation as a function of the stimuli impinging on political actors. The two classes of variables are the stimuli present in the environment and the stimuli the organism passes through its perceptual screen. Chapter III deals with participation as a function of personal factors: attitudes, beliefs, knowledge, and personality traits. Two chapters are devoted to environmental variables on which there has been more research. Participation as a function of political setting is discussed in Chapter IV, and participation as a function of social position is the subject of Chapter V. Political setting affects behavior partly through providing opportunities and setting boundaries and partly through the cognitive learning of the individual about his political world. Social position, too, provides opportunities, sets boundaries, and has an important impact on learning. In Chapter V, the impact of the standard demographic variables (age, sex, occupation, race, religion, and so on) is also examined. These variables are shorthand ways of talking about the differential impact of environment on learning; persons in the different categories used to classify these variables have grown up in different environments. In Chapter VI, a modest attempt is made to see what these findings mean for the functioning of the political system.

II

POLITICAL PARTICIPATION AS A FUNCTION OF STIMULI

THE CONCEPTUAL DIAGRAM (Figure 4 in Chapter I) indicates that before a political action can occur, the political actor must pick up relevant stimuli from the environment. Stimuli likely to be perceived as political make up only a small part of the total available. Persons vary considerably in the number they receive. A general proposition relating stimuli and political participation appears repeatedly in the research findings: **the more stimuli about politics a person receives, the greater the likelihood he will participate in politics, and the greater the depth of his participation** (Allardt & Pesonen, 1960; Almond & Verba, 1963; Berelson, et al., 1954; Campbell, 1962; Campbell, et al., 1954; Katz, 1957; Kyogoku & Ike, 1959; Lazarsfeld, et al., 1944; Lipset, 1960b; Marvick & Nixon, 1961; Pesonen, 1961; Rokkan & Campbell, 1960). Evidence supporting this proposition comes from at least twelve different studies and eight different countries: Finland, Germany, Italy, Japan, Mexico, Norway, Great Britain, and the United States.

This proposition should not be read to mean that reception of political stimuli causes political participation; it means only that the two are closely associated. We shall see later that **persons with a positive attraction to politics are more likely to receive stimuli about politics and to participate more.** Other research evidence suggests that *exposure to stimuli about politics increases the quantity and sharpness of political knowledge, stimulates interest, contributes to the decisiveness of political choices, and firms up attachment to a party or candi-*

date (Berelson, et al., 1954). There seems to be a circular pattern of relationships here that current research evidence does not enable us to untangle. Does an individual expose himself more to stimuli about politics because he is more interested in politics than others, or does he become more interested in politics as a result of lots of talk about politics in his environment? We know only that persons with high interest in, knowledge about, and exposure to politics are more likely to participate actively in politics.

Stimuli available in the environment of a political actor may come from the mass media, from campaign literature, from meetings, or from personal conversations. The tendency for those picking up more stimuli about politics to be more likely to be active in politics seems to hold regardless of the source of the stimuli. Personal contact and informal conversations are especially important stimuli for persons who are only marginally interested in politics. Several studies, from several countries, show that **persons participating in informal political discussions are more likely than nondiscussants to vote and participate in other ways in the political process** (Karlsson, 1958a; Kitt & Gleicher, 1950; Marvick & Nixon, 1961; Pesonen, 1961; Rokkan & Campbell, 1960).

The number of stimuli received and perceived as political is a function of two general factors: the number of stimuli about politics physically present in the environment and the operation of a person's perceptual screen, which picks up or shuts out stimuli about politics. We shall consider each of these general factors in turn.

EXPOSURE TO STIMULI AS A FUNCTION OF THEIR PRESENCE IN THE ENVIRONMENT

It is a truism that the greater the number of political stimuli available in the environment, the greater the likelihood that an individual will pick them up. The technological revolution in the mass media of communications has made political stimuli readily available to nearly every citizen of modern industrialized countries. Furthermore, the day is almost at hand when ubiquitous political stimuli, via the mass media, will be widely available in less developed areas. Whether the medium be radio, television, or newspapers seems to make little difference, except in countries with a high rate of illiteracy. Studies in the United States have shown that as media attention shifted from radio to television, more and more people received the greater proportion of their political information from television (Campbell, et al., 1954; Campbell, et al., 1960). Yet, the level of political interest and political activity remained approximately the same (Campbell, 1962). Technically, it is very easy now for candidates to reach a mass audience; an estimated 80 million Americans watched the first Kennedy-Nixon television debate in the campaign of 1960. This technology also makes it easier for citizens to become surfeited with political information. Thus, the problem of getting messages through to citizens may be no less complex than before.

The number of stimuli about politics available in the environment builds up cyclically to a climax just before an election and then declines. Political campaigns are made up almost totally of messages in one form or another. *As campaign messages increase, informal discussion about the messages also increases* (Berelson, et al., 1954); thus, campaigns have an accelerator effect on the total political stimuli available. In addition, at campaign time most parties make some attempt to contact at least some of the citizens personally about their vote intention. Personal-contact campaigns require a great amount of volunteer effort, and the nationwide coverage in the United States is generally less than 20 per cent.[1] The impact of personal contact is significant, however; **several studies show that citizens contacted personally are more likely to vote and to be interested in the campaign** (see Chapter IV).

Many societies also launch "get-out-the-vote campaigns" at election time. These presumably activate or reinforce citizen-duty beliefs and have at least some impact on the political activity level of the society, but we do not have really good

[1]Data are from the 1952 and 1956 election studies of the Survey Research Center, University of Michigan.

evidence about which types of appeals are most successful. So many factors influence a citizen's decision to vote that it is difficult to measure the independent contribution of a get-out-the-vote campaign.[2]

Even though political stimuli are generously available, there are important differences in their level from one environment to the next. We can speak here of the over-all politicization level of an individual's environment. **Middle-class persons are exposed to more stimuli about politics than working-class persons** (Berelson, et al., 1954; Eulau, 1962; Lazarsfeld, et al., 1944; M. Miller, 1952). **Men move in environments having more stimuli about politics than women do** (Berelson, et al., 1954; Gronseth, 1955; Lazarsfeld, et al., 1944). **Persons living in urbanized environments encounter more stimuli about politics than those living in the country** (Berelson, et al., 1954; Lazarsfeld, et al., 1944; Rokkan & Campbell, 1960). Campbell has ably summed up the latter point:

> City life is neither anonymous nor overwhelming to most people. On the contrary, city people seem to be subject to a much broader range of stimulation than rural people and are more responsive to it. Political involvement is consistently higher in the cities than it is in the countryside. There are many aspects of urban life which contribute to this relatively high level of interest but probably none is more important than the fact that the urban citizen is in constant contact with groups of people whom he may identify with and be influenced by, his neighbours, his work group, his union, his local party organization, and the like. Some of these groups have political relevance and they stimulate him politically (Campbell, 1962, p. 20).

Since persons tend to interact with other persons of about their own level of educational attainment, and since persons with higher education generally are more involved in and

---

[2] Some ingenious experiments attempting to measure this factor on the local level were carried out by Eldersveld (1956), Eldersveld & Dodge (1954), and Gosnell (1927).

talk more about politics, a more highly educated person encounters more stimuli about politics than one not so well educated (Almond & Verba, 1963; Berelson, et al., 1954; Converse & Dupeux, 1961; Converse & Dupeux, 1962; Lazarsfeld, et al., 1944; Lipset, 1960b; M. Miller, 1952). *Political conversation flows most naturally and freely when persons of the same sociocultural level interact* (Berelson, et al., 1954); ease of interaction is especially characteristic of "in-groups."

The most closely knit in-group of all is the family, and family experience has a profound impact on a person's exposure to political stimuli and on his activity level in politics. **Children growing up in a home with a high incidence of political discussion and a high intake level for political stimuli are more likely to maintain a high level of exposure to stimuli about politics when adults** (Berelson, et al., 1954; Marvick & Nixon, 1961; Rokkan & Campbell, 1960).

What little evidence we have suggests that the kinds of differences shown in politicization levels of personal environments for different sectors of society (class, sex, urban-rural, education, group membership) very likely are found in other political cultures as well as in the United States (studies from seven countries were cited above). There seem, however, to be over-all differences between national cultures as well. The five-nation survey showed that *persons living in Italy and Mexico tended to encounter many fewer stimuli about politics than persons living in Germany, the United Kingdom, and the United States* (Almond & Verba, 1963). A comparative study showed a greater incidence of newspaper reading in the United States than in France (Converse & Dupeux, 1962). Part of the difference vanished when statistical controls for education (higher in the United States) were applied, but highly educated Americans more universally read newspapers than highly educated Frenchmen. These two studies suggest that **politicization levels are different from country to country** and that the level in the United States is higher than in most other Western countries, although the level in Britain is close behind.

EXPOSURE TO STIMULI AS A FUNCTION OF A PERSON'S PERCEPTUAL SCREEN

Even persons living in the same environment expose themselves to differing numbers of stimuli about politics. This could only mean that some persons are picking up the available stimuli, whereas others are shutting them out. The operation of an individual's perceptual screen was discussed in Chapter I. A point made there bears repeating here: the perceptual screen operates to protect the organism from an overload of stimuli. Overload can occur in two ways: the total amount can be so excessive that all messages are garbled (like a radio tuned to several stations at once); or the stimuli hammer so incessantly that the senses are dulled (like the villagers' reaction to the boy who cried wolf too often).

There are important individual differences in the ability to encode political messages and in the ability to sustain political interest. Therefore, the likelihood that the perceptual screen will let political messages through is a function of personal abilities and needs. The screen also operates to protect the individual from stimuli which threaten his security system. Uncongenial or threatening messages either may be shut out entirely or may be distorted to soften the potential damage. The operation of a given person's perceptual screen is unique to his personality. Despite this uniqueness, aggregates of persons follow certain discernable patterns.

Persons who are attracted to politics (interested, concerned, curious, intense preferences) **expose themselves more to stimuli about politics than those not so attracted** (Allardt & Pesonen 1960; Berelson, et al., 1954; Lane, 1959; Lazarsfeld, et al., 1944; Pesonen, 1960; Pesonen, 1961). This proposition has been found almost universally in studies gathering the relevant data. It is so close to being a truism that few researchers bother any more to investigate it or report it. The relationship is important, however, in that any effort to increase the political information level of the populace must find some way to gain and maintain the interest of citizens. Disinterested and surfeited persons do not pick up political stimuli. Persons not attending to politics are called "parochials" in the five-nation study; their incidence is much greater in Italy and Mexico than in Germany, the United Kingdom, and the United States (Almond & Verba, 1963, Ch. 3).

A related proposition is that **persons with strong preferences for a party or candidate pick up more political stimuli than those with weak preferences** (Allardt & Pesonen, 1960, Campbell, et al., 1954; Campbell, et al., 1960; Lazarsfeld, et al., 1944). **Even if his mind is made up, the strong partisan exposes himself to more stimuli about politics than the undecided,** who, objectively, may need more information (Lazarsfeld, et al., 1944; Milne & Mackenzie, 1954). The partisan is not really interested in messages from both sides; **primarily, partisans pick up messages from their own side** (Lazarsfeld, et al., 1944; Milne & Mackenzie, 1954; Pesonen, 1960; Ziff, 1948).

Additional evidence that the disposition to seek political stimuli is a personality trait comes from the finding that **political information-seeking behavior is cumulative** (Berelson, et al., 1954; Katz, 1947; Lane 1959; Lazarsfeld, et al., 1944; Pesonen, 1960; Pesonen, 1961; Scheuch, 1961). **The same persons have high exposure to several different kinds of media, and their high exposure continues throughout the surge and decline of political campaigns.** The behavior is cumulative in another way; **persons exposing themselves highly to political stimuli also expose themselves highly to nonpolitical stimuli** (Berelson, et al., 1954; Katz, 1947; Lane, 1959; Lazarsfeld, et al., 1944; Pesonen, 1960; Pesonen, 1961; Scheuch, 1961).

Persons pick up or seek stimuli about politics for a variety of purposes: to fill a need for knowledge, to satisfy their curiosity, to help solve problems, to fulfill the sense of duty that a good citizen must be informed. But why do some persons deliberately shut out stimuli about politics? Research evidence on that question is relatively inadequate. The theory set forth in Chapter I leads to speculation that the perceptual screen shuts out stimuli as a way of protecting the personality (ego) of the individual. **Persons who lack education and sophistication about politics tend to shut out political stimuli** (Almond & Verba, 1963; Berelson, et al., 1954; Converse & Dupeux, 1961; Converse & Dupeux, 1962; Lazarsfeld, et al., 1944; Lipset, 1960b; M. Miller, 1952) as a way of protecting themselves from messages which they do not understand and cannot absorb. **Persons of middle age,** presumably with greater understanding of politics, **expose themselves to more stimuli about politics than persons of young ages do** (Berelson, et al.; 1954; Lazarsfeld, et al., 1944). *"Busy" persons,* who perceive themselves as having no spare time for politics, *protect themselves from political stimuli which are irrelevant to their pressing concerns.* If political stimuli are present in excessive numbers, some must be shut out to make the others intelligible. Messages which threaten the ego must be shut out or distorted so that their potential damage is diminished.

Evidence presented by one scholar suggests why certain persons hesitate to discuss politics: *persons with weak egos shun the clash of political argument because of the threat of deflation of their ego* (Rosenberg 1954-1955; Rosenberg, 1962). Contrariwise, *persons with high self-esteem welcome political discussion and expose themselves readily to political stimuli. Some persons believe they will lose friends or opportunities for business success if they discuss politics.* Not all exposure to stimuli about politics requires engaging in a discussion; thus, the propositions are not directly on the point of this section. However, the more general point is relevant: many persons perceive politics as threatening and may well be inclined to shut political stimuli out of their lives.

Political stimuli also may be shut out because they are lost in the general competition for a given individual's attention. Persons attend to only one message at a time, and the choice of message to be focused on is dependent on the predispositional complex of the reacting individual. A predisposition to select out political messages rarely has highest priority for ordinary citizens. At campaign time, the predisposition may be high for those who are interested in politics. Exciting or unique political events stand out enough so that even some of the disinterested pick up messages about them. As a rule, however, ordinary political stimuli do not compete adequately with other possible messages for the attention of the average citizen. Only a small proportion of the population have learned to pick up and enjoy political messages; their predispositional complex gives such messages high priority. By and large, these same persons are those most likely to become active in politics.

III

POLITICAL PARTICIPATION AS A FUNCTION OF PERSONAL FACTORS

THE CONCEPTUAL DIAGRAM (Figure 4, Chapter I) isolates five "personal" factors, three of which have been related in research to political behavior: attitudes, beliefs, and personality traits. (There has been almost no research relating heredity or physiological and psychological needs to political behavior.) In discussing that diagram, we defined attitudes as a positive or negative valence between actor and object. We defined belief as a cognition with an extra feeling of credibility. These two are predispositions "up close" to behavior. Personality was conceived as a more general background factor or disposition which feeds into a cognitive framework and finds expression as a belief or attitude.

It is virtually impossible to measure any of these personal factors directly; their presence and character can only be inferred from behavior in response to a stimulus. Typically, an experimenter or an interviewer gives some sort of verbal stimulus to a respondent and then measures or records the behavior that stimulus elicits. In the case of an attitude measure, he may read a series of statements to the respondent and ask him to agree or disagree with them. The inferential leap from response to attitude seems to be justified so long as one can be reasonably certain that the respondent is not lying. Personality traits are measured in much the same way as attitudes, except that a longer and less certain inferential leap is required. The stimuli used in personality measures ask about behavior in certain kinds of situations; they also ask for attitudes and beliefs. From these bits of evidence, the presence or absence of a trait is inferred.

Because of these measurement difficulties, it is important for the reader to keep in mind a distinction between a theoretical conceptualization of a factor and its operational definition (measuring instrument). A researcher always has a theoretical conception of a factor in mind as he works with it. For example, it may be a concept like "effectiveness." A major challenge facing him is to try to devise a measuring instrument (a scale, an index, an item) which will create in the mind of his respondent the same kind of concept that is in his own mind. This process is called operationalizing, and the measure he creates can be called his operational definition of his concept. It is a well-known fact that words don't always mean the same thing from person to person, and thus it is almost impossible to duplicate accurately a theoretical concept in a measuring instrument. The researcher works by trial and error to sharpen the measuring instrument so that it is the closest possible approximation to his theoretical concept. He knows he is getting closer when the measure seems stable in repeated applications over time, and when it relates to other variables in a manner that his theory leads him to expect. But there is always the possibility that the measure he has created is, in reality, somewhat different from his theoretical conception of the factor. This difficulty affects the following discussion in two ways.

Many times it seems, theoretically, that a very close relationship should exist between two variables, but the correlation shown in the data is relatively low. This can mean that the actual relationship is much lower than expected, but it can also mean that the measuring instruments are so imperfect that no higher relationship could be found. Thus, every finding is subject to two interpretations: that the real world is accurately mirrored in the data, or that the measuring instruments are so poor that the data do not reflect the real world. For example, one might hypothesize, theoretically, that persons with dominant personality traits would be more likely to become active in politics than persons who are less dominant. When a dominance scale is administered to a group of actives and nonactives, there seems to be no difference between the two groups on the incidence of dominant personalities. Does this mean that dominants are not more likely to enter politics than nondominants, or does it mean that the scale does not measure dominance, as had been supposed? The challenge to the social scientist is to try several approaches and extract knowledge from such imperfect data. Difficulties in operationalization also affect the classification of variables into the three sections of this chapter. Despite our theoretical effort to distinguish attitude, belief, and personality, many operationally defined variables overlap our conceptual boundaries. A given variable is discussed under a particular heading because the main emphasis of what is measured fell in that category. No effort is made to justify particular classifications, since that is not crucial to the intellectual enterprise of this book. The reader also will encounter several instances of interrelationship of beliefs, attitudes, and personality traits. In certain cases, it is difficult to sort out cause from effect.

PARTICIPATION AS A FUNCTION OF ATTITUDE AND ATTITUDE INTENSITY

Political attitudes are cognitions about and positive or negative feelings toward political objects. These feelings have both direction (for or against a particular policy, candidate, or party) and intensity. Some of the difficulties involved in generalizing about direction of preferences were discussed in Chapter I. It was pointed out, and bears repeating, that there is such a large amount of evidence on the direction of political attitudes that reviewing it and attempting to explain directional preferences would take us far beyond the scope of this book. Intensity of attitude feelings, however, is more germane to explaining why people get involved in politics: it determines how vigorously the political object will be supported or opposed.

Just as psychological involvement (interest in and concern about politics) is a central variable determining exposure to political stimuli, so is it a central attitudinal variable relating to participation in politics. Persons have a general valence (positive or negative) toward politics. At least nine studies in four or more countries (the relationship is so regular that

TABLE III. 1
Percentage at Different Levels of Political Participation by Level of Psychological Involvement in the 1956 Election [a]

| Campaign Activity Index | Psychological Involvement Index (%) (Combination of Interest in Election and Care Who Wins) | | | | |
	Highest		Lowest		
	1	2	3	4	Total
Nonvoter	9	20	30	47	25
Spectator activities only	64	66	61	49	61
At least one gladitorial activity	27	14	9	4	14
Total	100	100	100	100	100
Number of cases	(436)	(542)	(458)	(335)	(1,771)
Tau beta correlation = .29					

[a]Data are from the 1956 study of the American electorate conducted by the Survey Research Center, University of Michigan.

many authors do not bother to report it) have shown that persons who are more interested in or concerned about an election are more likely to vote (Benny, et al., 1956; Berelson, et al., 1954; Campbell, et al., 1954; Campbell, et al., 1960; Janowitz & Marvick, 1956; Karlsson, 1958a; Kitt & Gleicher, 1950; Kuroda, 1964; Lazarsfeld, et al., 1944; M. Miller, 1952; Pesonen, 1960; Särlvik, 1961a). Furthermore, persons who are more psychologically involved in politics are more likely to engage in political and campaign activities beyond voting (Campbell, et al., 1954; Campbell, et al., 1960; Kuroda, 1964; Lazarsfeld, et al., 1944; Pesonen, 1960; Pesonen, 1961; Saenger, 1945).

Some actual data showing a relationship between psychological involvement and a campaign activity index are set forth in Table III.1. The Psychological Involvement Index was developed from answers to questions asking how interested the respondent was in the election and whether he cared who won. The Campaign Activity Index was developed from questions asking respondents simply if they did or did not perform seven political acts in the current campaign: vote, wear a button or sticker, try to talk someone into voting a certain way, give money to a party or candidate, attend a party or campaign meeting, join a political club, or do some work for a party or candidate.[1]

Persons who had not voted and had not performed any of the other political activities were placed in the nonvoter category; this would correspond to our apathetics. Spectator activities include voting, attempting to talk others into voting a certain way (proselyting), and displaying a button or sticker. Persons who had joined a political club, given money, attended meetings, or worked in the campaign were classified as gladiators. This somewhat broader definition of gladiatorial activities than that given in Chapter I was used to obtain sufficient cases for statistical analysis in the gladiatorial category. If we had adhered to the strict definition given in Chapter I, less than 1 per cent could have been classified as full-fledged gladiators. The data were coded to pick out persons who performed two or more gladiatorial activities, but this tighter definition produced no significant alteration in the analysis.

The reader can see in the table that at higher levels of psychological involvement, the percentage of nonvoters is smaller and the percentage of gladiators is larger. The tau beta correlation of the two variables is .29, which is as strong a relationship with participation as is shown by any other independent variable.[2] Only about one-fourth of the American electorate could be considered highly involved in the election by the measure shown in the table. A study conducted in Elmira, New York, reported about one-third of the electorate as greatly interested in the election and about one-fifth as believing it would make a good deal of difference who won (Berelson, et al., 1954).

The intensity of one's attraction to a party, a candidate, or an issue is also related to political participation. At least nine studies in three or more countries have shown that **persons who strongly identify with or intensely prefer a given party are more likely to participate actively in the political process** (Berelson, 1949; Campbell, et al., 1954; Campbell, et al., 1960; Campbell & Valen, 1961; Hastings, 1954; Marvick &

---

[1] See the appendix for details of the development of the indices.

[2] The tau beta is a nonparametric statistic which is a conservative estimate of the Pearson r.

Nixon, 1961; Pesonen, 1960; Pesonen, 1961; Saenger, 1945). Persons with intense preferences are especially likely to proselytize others, but they are more likely than those with weak preferences to carry out other political activities as well. As might be expected, **those with intense preferences are also highly likely to be interested in politics** (Berelson, et al., 1954; Campbell, et al., 1954; Campbell, et al., 1960; Pesonen, 1960; Pesonen, 1961; Särlvik, 1961a). Strength of partisan preference seems to be a function of other variables, too. *Older persons tend to have stronger party preferences than younger* (Campbell & Valen, 1961). This age-partisanship relationship seems more to be a function of the length of time a person has identified with a party and the length of his residence in his community than it is of aging per se (Campbell, et al., 1960, p. 164). *Long identification with a party and long residence in a community tend to encourage strong partisanship. Farm residents in the United States tend to have less intense partisan preferences than city residents* (Campbell, et al., 1960).

The same basic generalization applies to candidate and issue preference as to partisan preference. Several studies have shown that **persons with intense preferences for candidates or issues are more likely to be active in politics** (Campbell, et al., 1954; Campbell, et al., 1960; Marvick & Nixon, 1961). *If a person's issue preferences pull in different directions* (one issue toward one party and another issue toward another party), *the likelihood of his participation in politics is lessened* (Campbell et al., 1954; Campbell, et al., 1960). Conversely, *congruence in direction of political attitudes* (preferences for party, candidate, and issues) *increases the probability of participation* (Lane, 1959).

Why is it that some persons become highly involved psychologically in politics, or have intense preferences (or both, since they are highly correlated), while others do not? The difference stems partly from differences in social position and partly from differing personality development. Personality correlates are treated later in this chapter; only social-position factors are discussed here. **Persons of higher socioeconomic status (SES), especially higher education, are more likely to become highly involved psychologically in politics than per-**

sons of lower status (Benny & Geiss, 1950; Benny, et al., 1956; Berelson, et al., 1954; Campbell, 1962; Campbell, et al., 1954; Campbell, et al., 1960; Converse & Dupeux, 1961; Eulau, 1962; Lazarsfeld, et al., 1944; Saenger, 1945).

> Perhaps the surest single predictor of political involvement is number of years of formal education. There are apathetic college graduates and highly involved people of very low educational level but the over-all relationship of education and political interest is impressive. It is impossible to say with confidence why it is that formal schooling makes people more responsive to political stimulation. One may surmise that education tends to widen the scope of one's acquaintance with political facts, to increase capacity to perceive the personal implications of political events, or to enlarge one's confidence in his own ability to act effectively politically. Whatever the precise nature of the educational process, it has clear effects on political interest (Campbell, 1962, p. 20).

It is traditional in most cultures that politics is the primary concern of men, and that women should follow the male political lead. The social changes wrought by modern industrial society are eroding this sex difference, but the impact of the tradition is still visible. **Men are more likely to be psychologically involved in politics than women** (Benny & Geiss, 1950; Berelson, et al., 1954; Lazarsfeld, et al., 1944). This difference is more pronounced at the lower educational levels than at the upper, where it is nearly obliterated in modern industrial societies (Campbell, et al., 1960, p. 489; Rokkan & Campbell, 1960). In the United States, females seem especially low on interest in political issues but seem somewhat more oriented to candidates than men; there is no difference between the sexes on the intensity of their partisanship (Almond & Verba, 1963; Campbell, et al., 1954; Campbell, et al., 1960). In Germany, Britain, Mexico, and Italy, women are less likely to feel psychologically involved in politics than men; the sex difference is especially striking in Italy (Almond & Verba, 1963; Benny, et al., 1956).

Some studies have shown that *older persons are more interested in politics than younger* (Berelson, et al., 1954; Lazarsfeld, et al., 1944). However, this relationship, like the relationship between age and partisanship, may be a function of length of identification with a party, length of residence in a community, and the acquisition of property and family responsibilities. Mere aging would not seem to produce increased interest. A study in Greenwich, England, found no relationship between age and political interest (Benny, et al., 1956).

The social group with which a person identifies and interacts can have an impact on interest in politics. Some studies have shown that *members of labor unions, especially those who identify strongly with the union, are more interested in politics than nonmembers or weakly identified members* (Benny, et al., 1956; Kornhauser, et al., 1956). Other studies have shown that religious-group membership is related to political interest. *Jews generally have higher political interest levels than Catholics or Protestants* (Saenger, 1945). *Persons belonging to two or more groups which pull in different directions* (cross-pressured persons) *are likely to have diminished political interest* (Lazarsfeld, et al., 1944; Lipset, 1960b).

Interest connotes a positive attraction to politics, but what of the politically dissatisfied? Do they jump into the fray and try to change things, or do they sulk on the sidelines and only complain? Research evidence on this point is not conclusive. A study in the United States showed that *nonvoters were less likely to be dissatisfied with political conditions than voters and were less likely to welcome changes in the political structure* (Connelly & Field, 1944). Others have speculated that the dissatisfied citizens were more likely to become active (Pesonen, 1961; Rosenberg, 1954-1955). It is probably necessary for the person to see some relationship between political activity and solution to his problems. *Persons who were highly anxious and were absorbed in their personal problems were found to be unlikely to be interested in politics.*[3]

Campbell (1962) speculated that both those persons with little political frustration and also those with great frustration, who may be immobilized by it, are likely to be apathetic. The person who is moderately frustrated about politics has a

[3]Goldhamer (1950), Lane (1959), Mussen & Wyszynski (1952), and Rosenberg (1962) expound much the same hypothesis.

TABLE III. 2

Percentage at Different Levels of Political Participation
by Rank on the Efficacy Scale [a]

| | Rank on Efficacy Scale (%) | | | | | |
| | Lowest | | | | Highest | |
Campaign Activity Index	0	1	2	3	4	Total
Nonvoter	46	38	23	15	6	25
Spectator activities only	51	54	65	64	66	61
At least one gladiatorial activity	3	8	12	21	28	14
Total	100	100	100	100	100	100
Number of cases	(265)	(343)	(463)	(503)	(197)	(1,771)

[a]Data are from the 1956 study of the American electorate conducted by the Survey Research Center, University of Michigan.

motive to become active and is not immobilized by his emotions. Lane (1959) has suggested that hostility and inner conflict may be displaced into the political sphere and result in support of extremist political movements. Each hypothesis in this and the preceding paragraph has some evidence to support it; more is needed, however, to provide a satisfactory level of confidence.

Persons who believe they can accomplish things through politics could be said to have a positive attitude toward it. Such persons feel efficacious about political action, and an efficacy scale has been devised to measure this feeling.[4] Not surprisingly, a feeling of efficacy is related to psychological involvement in politics; **persons who are psychologically involved in politics are more likely to feel efficacious about political action** (Berelson, et al., 1954; Campbell, et al., 1954; Campbell, et al., 1960). Table III.2 shows a cross-tabulation of the efficacy scale with the Campaign Activity Index, described above.

The table clearly indicates that **persons who feel efficacious politically are much more likely to become actively involved in politics** (Almond & Verba, 1963, all five nations;

[4] It was devised by the Political Behavior research team at the Survey Research Center, University of Michigan. Campbell, et al. (1954); Campbell, et al. (1960). See the appendix for details on the scale.

Berelson, et al., 1954; Campbell, et al., 1954; Campbell, et al., 1960; Dahl, 1961; Jensen, 1960). The relationship persists with a significant tau beta correlation of about .27 even when statistical controls for response set are applied. A study in Evanston, Illinois, shows a very similar correlation (Jensen, 1960). Some persons answer questions or items in a set way (such as agreeing with every item) instead of responding to the content of the item; this response set can bias results seriously. Researchers try to account for this bias in examining their results, and this is especially important when dealing with attitudinal and personality scales.[5]

The efficacy scale was cross-tabulated separately with all of the specific activities included in the Campaign Activity Index. Generally, the efficacy scale showed a stronger relationship with spectator activities (voting, proselyting, and wearing a button) than with gladiator activities (giving money, attending meetings, joining a club, and working in a campaign).[6] Giving money and attending meetings (which are transitional activities and have a higher percentage of persons doing them) showed a higher correlation with efficacy than working in a campaign or joining a political club. One would have to conclude, however, that a feeling of efficacy facilitates participation in nearly any type of political activity.

What factors tend to develop a sense of political efficacy in a person? **Several studies in several nations have shown that upper SES persons, especially the better educated, are more likely to develop efficacious feelings** (Almond & Verba, 1963, all five nations; Campbell, et al., 1954; Campbell, et al., 1960; Dahl, 1961; Eulau, 1962; Litt, 1963). Quite understandably, a person who knows more about the political world is more likely to feel that he can do something to manipulate it.[7] **In addition, he sees other persons in his social milieu take political action with the obvious expectation that they will get results.**

[5] For a discussion of this problem and some interesting correlates of response set, see Milbrath (1962).

[6] Almond & Verba (1963), using a different scale (but similar conceptually), also found in five countries a higher correlation with spectator than with gladiator activities.

[7] This is not always true; he could know enough to decide that efforts at manipulation do not bear sufficient returns for the work required.

Dahl has hypothesized that participation in politics and feelings of efficacy feed on each other, producing a circularity of effects. Persons with middle-class resources more likely participate in politics and more likely feel efficacious about political action. Their political participation probably increases their sense of efficacy, and their sense of efficacy, in turn, probably increases their participation. In contrast, persons with working-class resources are less likely to participate in politics and less likely to feel efficacious about political action. Their failure to participate contributes to their sense of political impotence, and their lack of a sense of efficacy increases the probability that they will not participate (Dahl, 1961). This reasoning receives indirect support from another study, which found that *persons who were personally contacted by a canvasser were more likely to feel efficacious than those not so contacted* (Eldersveld, 1956).

Whether or not a person develops a feeling of political efficacy and competence depends a great deal on the type of political culture in which he lives. The five-nation study showed that **persons living in the United States and the United Kingdom were much more likely to develop a sense of political competence than persons living in Germany, Mexico, and Italy. Persons living in Italy were especially unlikely to develop a feeling of competence (Almond & Verba, 1963, Ch.7). Males also were more likely to develop a feeling of efficacy in all five countries** (Almond & Verba, 1963; Campbell, et al., 1954). United States data show that *white persons and city dwellers are more likely to develop a sense of efficacy* (Campbell, et al., 1954). Some recent data lead us to suspect, however, that dwellers in cities where politics are dominated by a political machine are not likely to develop a sense of political efficacy (Litt, 1963). *Persons living in the American South are less likely to develop a sense of political efficacy than persons living in other sections of the country* (Campbell, et al., 1954).[8] Age does not show a consistent relationship to a sense of efficacy.

The researchers who designed the efficacy scale wanted

[8]See Milbrath (1965) for documentation showing the lower political activity level of the American South.

to see if they could find a more general personality trait that lay behind a sense of political efficacy. They designed a new personality scale they called the "Personal Effectiveness Scale." Unlike the efficacy scale, which asked about a respondent's attraction to or repulsion from political participation, this one has no mention of politics in the items. Here is the way its principal designer has described it:

> It is our assumption that people begin at an early age to develop a sense of their own capacity to manage the world around them. We think that some people develop a self-confident, positive attitude with which they meet the problems of every-day life while others see themselves as characteristically giving way in the face of environmental pressure, unable to manage the conflicting forces which they encounter. We expect to find this trait related to a variety of other psychological characteristics, among them specifically, political involvement (Campbell, 1962, p. 12).[9]

As the designers expected, there was a high correlation between the personal effectiveness scale and the efficacy scale (Campbell, et al., 1960, p.517). As Table III.3 shows, the new scale is also clearly related to the Campaign Activity Index. **Persons who feel more effective in their everyday tasks and challenges are more likely to participate in politics** (Allport, 1945; Campbell, 1962; Campbell, et al., 1960; Dahl, 1961; Lane, 1959; Mussen & Wyszinski, 1952). The relationship between personal effectiveness and political participation remains significant when controls for response-set bias are applied. Personal effectiveness seems to show a higher correlation with participation for persons with low education than for those with high education. The highly educated person probably has other factors in his environment that may push him into politics even if he has a low feeling of effectiveness. The poorly educated person, however, is likely to feel very little "push" from his environment to become active in politics and is very dependent on his personal sense of effectiveness to open the way for his participation. As with the efficacy scale, the personal effectiveness scale shows a higher corre-

[9] For a list of items and other details about the scale see the appendix.

TABLE III. 3
Percentage at Different Levels of Participation by Position on the Personal Effectiveness Scale [a]

	Rank on Personal Effectiveness Scale (%)[b]			
	Low	Medium	High	Total
Campaign Activity Index	0–1	2–3	4	
Nonvoters	54	24	12	24
Spectator activities only	40	65	66	62
At least one gladitorial activity	6	11	22	14
Total	100	100	100	100
Number of cases	(93)	(285)	(204)	(582)

tau beta correlation = .28

[a]Data are from the 1956 study of the American electorate conducted by the Survey Research Center, University of Michigan.
[b]This scale was administered to only one-third of the full national sample, thus the total N is considerably less than in other tables.

lation with spectator activities, like voting, than it does with gladiatorial activities (Campbell, 1962; Campbell, et al., 1960).

Other personality traits, as well, seem to relate to a sense of political efficacy. *Persons high in political efficacy are more likely to be trusting of politics and politicians* (Agger, et al., 1961; Litt, 1963). A study in Boston showed, however, that this relationship did not hold in a city dominated by a political machine; no matter how efficacious persons felt about political action, they still didn't trust politicians (Litt, 1963). The expected relationship between trust and efficacy was found in Boston suburbs, however. This general relationship makes sense in this way: if a person believes that politics responds to the efforts of persons like himself, he is less likely to distrust the motives and actions of politicians.

A sense of duty to participate in politics is another important political attitude relating to participation. Although a sizable percentage of persons feel such a duty, the feeling is by no means universal and probably not as widespread as one might suppose. The five-nation study showed that 40 per cent of the respondents in the United States felt they had a duty

TABLE III. 4

Percentage at Different Levels of Political Participation by Rank on the Citizen Duty Scale [a]

| | Citizen Duty Scale (%) | | | | | |
| | Low | | | | High | |
Campaign Activity Index	0	1	2	3	4	Total
Nonvoters	82	57	45	23	13	25
Spectator activities only	15	42	48	63	68	61
At least one gladiatorial activity	3	1	7	14	19	14
Total	100	100	100	100	100	100
Number of cases	(91)	(78)	(145)	(641)	(817)	(1,772)

[a]Data are from the 1956 study of the American electorate conducted by the Survey Research Center, University of Michigan.

to vote (Almond & Verba, 1963, p. 171). The percentages in the other countries were: United Kingdom, 18; Germany, 15; Italy, 2; Mexico, 1. About 20 per cent in the United States and the United Kingdom felt they had a duty to participate in local government activities; the percentages were even lower in the other three countries. A much smaller percentage felt they had a duty to take part in the activities of political parties: the 6 per cent who felt so in the United States was the highest of the nations; three others had 4 or 5 per cent; and Italy had only 1 per cent (Almond & Verba, 1963, p. 171). What little sense of citizen duty is felt seems, then, to be confined to spectator activities with relatively little carry-over to gladiatorial activities.

Feeling a duty to participate seems to carry over to political action: several studies show that **persons feeling a duty to participate are more likely to do so** (Campbell, et al., 1954; Campbell, et al., 1960; Jensen, 1960; Marvick & Nixon, 1961; Mayntz, 1961). The researchers at the Survey Research Center designed a scale to measure the duty a person feels to vote, and rank on this scale is cross-tabulated with the Campaign Activity Index in Table III.4.[10] The tendency for those with a high sense of duty to be more likely to participate is clear in

[10] For details on the scale see the appendix.

TABLE III. 5

Sense of Civic Duty among Party Actives and the General Citizenry [a]

I think that everyone has a duty to be active in politics		General Citizenry	Party Actives	Total
	Disagree	31 (24%)	2 (4%)	33 (19%)
	Agree	96 (76%)	44 (96%)	140 (81%)
	Total	127 (100%)	46 (100%)	173 (100%)
		correlation significant at .01		
I think that one fulfills his civic duty if he votes regularly				
	Disagree	26 (21%)	18 (39%)	44 (26%)
	Agree	100 (79%)	28 (61%)	128 (74%)
	Total	126 (100%)	46 (100%)	172 (100%)
		correlation significant at .05		

[a]Data are from a survey in Evanston, Illinois, conducted by a graduate seminar at Northwestern University (Jensen, 1960).

the table. The trend is most clear for voting, dropping from a high of 82 per cent nonvoters at the low end of the scale to 13 per cent nonvoters at the high end. The rise of gladiatorial activities from the low to the high end is only from 3 to 19 per cent. The corresponding rise for the efficacy scale is from 3 to 28 per cent. This evidence indirectly supports the point that very few persons feel a duty to participate in gladiatorial activities.

Some data gathered by a graduate seminar at Northwestern University not only tend to confirm this but also illustrate how one must be cautious in framing questions about attitudes. The seminar asked a sample of party actives and a sample of citizens from Evanston, Illinois, to agree or disagree with these two statements: "I think everyone has a duty to be active in politics." and "I think that one fulfills his civic duty if he votes regularly." The responses of the two samples to these two items are shown in Table III.5 The striking thing is that a majority of both samples agreed with both statements. The feeling of duty to be active was nearly universal among party actives but was also strongly supported among the general citizenry. Yet, the feeling that one's duty is fulfilled if he votes was almost as strongly supported; even a majority of the party actives agreed with the statement. The general and greater tendency for party actives to express a duty to take political action is clear in both questions.

Feelings of citizen duty are instilled by the political socialization process and have their roots both in society and in personality. The data from the five-nation study cited above clearly indicate that some political cultures more probably instill this sense of duty than others. The directors of the study checked carefully to make sure that the differences found between countries were not simply an artifact of differences in education, status, or role between the countries. Statistical controls for education, occupation, and sex were applied to the national differences in sense of duty, but the latter persisted despite these controls (Almond & Verba, 1963, pp. 176-177).

These control factors (social-position factors within a nation) have an impact, too. The citizen-duty attitude relates to many of the same social-position variables as the political-efficacy attitude. **Upper-socioeconomic-status persons, especially those with higher education, are more likely to develop a sense of citizen duty** (Almond & Verba, 1963; Campbell, et al., 1954; Campbell, et al., 1960; Eulau, 1962). Some scholars have speculated that middle-class society especially facilitates the development of conscience and duty. Not only does the middle class instill duty to society as a value in its children, but conformity pressures within that stratum help to enforce the code (Riesman, 1950; Lane, 1959).

White persons and city dwellers, in the United States, *are more likely to develop a sense of citizen duty* (Campbell, et al., 1954).[11] *Persons growing up in the American South are less likely to develop it* (Campbell, et al., 1954). In the United States, there is very little age or sex difference in likelihood of developing a sense of duty (Almond & Verba, 1963; Campbell, et al., 1954). In the other four nations included in the five-nation study, however, the difference between men and women (men higher) in likelihood of developing a sense of civic

[11] The generalization may hold in other countries as well, but no data exist to confirm or deny.

duty was more pronounced (Almond & Verba, 1963, p. 177).

The psychological mechanisms by which conscience and duty are instilled into personality are so complex and incompletely understood that it would be inappropriate to attempt full exposition here. A child learns what his duty is by both tuition and example. In Western society, most citizens learn early that they have a duty to study politics and to pass judgment on political actions. This sense of duty may well be important in recruiting sufficient workers to keep the political system functioning.

PARTICIPATION AS A FUNCTION OF COGNITIONS AND BELIEFS

Citizens vary considerably in the sophistication of their conceptions about politics and government. These differences can be measured in several ways: (1) the amount of political knowledge held; (2) the accuracy of the knowledge; (3) the number of issues on which a person has opinions; (4) the ability to relate positions on issues to the stands of parties and candidates; and (5) the ability to see the relationships between issue positions so that they form a consistent political philosophy. This last could be called the ability to think in an ideological framework, and only a relatively small proportion of persons in any political society could be said to have it. Using a much less stringent conception of ideological thinking than this, a study of the 1956 presidential election in the United States found only 11.5 per cent of the adult population able to achieve an "ideological" level of conceptualization about politics (Campbell, et al., 1960, p. 249). Even if one looks simply for accuracy of information about politics, most studies find that only 10 to 20 per cent of the population know their politics well.

No matter how political sophistication is measured, it shows impressive correlations with participation in politics. **The more sophisticated a person's cognitions and beliefs about politics, the greater the likelihood of his participation in the political process** (Agger & Ostrom, 1956; Campbell, et al., 1954; Campbell, et al., 1960; Campbell & Kahn, 1952; Connelly & Field, 1944; Eldersveld, 1956; Hastings, 1954; Jensen, 1960; Korchin, 1946; Karlsson, 1958a; Marvick & Nixon, 1961; M. Miller, 1952; Särlvik, 1961a). The relationship comes into sharper focus if one thinks about lack of knowledge as a barrier to participation. A person is naturally reluctant to become involved if he does not understand how a system functions or how he might relate to it. Respondents in a study of political participation in Evanston, Illinois, were asked if they perceived any advantages and any disadvantages in taking part in politics. Party actives not only perceived more advantages to participation but also more disadvantages than did the general citizenry (Jensen, 1960).

Knowledge and understanding, then, are necessary but not sufficient conditions for political action. In a survey of information and attitudes on world affairs conducted in Albany, New York, in 1949, by the Survey Research Center, it was found that 32 per cent of the respondents believed that writing to a congressman was one way that ordinary citizens could influence the government. Yet, only 11 per cent of the sample reported that they had written such a letter (cited in Key, 1961, pp. 418-419). Note not only the differential between those who know they can and those who do, but also the fact that only 32 per cent mentioned a letter to a congressman as an efficacious political action.

Some scholars have suggested that as politics becomes increasingly complex, fewer people will understand it, and the proportion of apathetics will increase (Riesman & Glazer, 1950). This is a reasonable hypothesis if politics is so complex that the average person cannot understand it even if he tries. However, other research evidence suggests that an impoverished conceptual structure of politics is as much or more a function of lack of interest as it is of increasing complexity of the subject. **Several studies have found a significant positive correlation between interest in and knowledge about politics** (Campbell, et al., 1954; Campbell, et al., 1960; Lazarsfeld, et al., 1944; Pesonen, 1961). **Strong partisanship,** which correlates positively with interest, **also correlates positively with knowledge of politics** (Campbell, et al., 1954; Campbell, et al., 1960; Lazarsfeld, et al., 1944; Pesonen,

TABLE III. 6

Percentage at Different Levels of Political Participation by Degree of Familiarity with Issues [a]

	Issue Familiarity (Number of Issues on Which Respondent Held Opinions)				
Campaign Activity Index	7 or fewer	8-10	11-13	14-16	Total
Nonvoters	45	26	18	14	25
Spectator activities only	49	61	67	65	61
At least one gladiatorial activity	6	13	15	21	14
Total	100	100	100	100	100
Number of cases	(448)	(330)	(436)	(557)	(1,771)

[a]Data are from the 1956 study of the American electorate conducted by the Survey Research Center, University of Michigan.

1961). Strong partisanship not only inclines a person to pay more attention to politics and thus pick up more information, it also inclines him to accept the party interpretation of political events. Having a readymade (by the party) interpretation makes it easier for the partisan to put doubts aside and plunge into action. Saenger (1945) hypothesized that persons who do not recognize party differences on issues probably are more open to personal and group influences.

Gladiators generally have more knowledge about politics than spectators who, in turn, have more knowledge than apathetics. Substantiation for this point is given in Table III.6, where the Campaign Activity Index is cross-tabulated with an Issue Familiarity Index.[12] Respondents were questioned about their position on sixteen issues. The index is created from a simple count of the number of issues with which they were familiar.

If gladiators have opinions on more issues, does it follow that they are more likely to be motivated by ideological concerns than spectators? The evidence on this is inconclusive. A study in Elmira, New York, showed that party workers were no more likely to be motivated by ideological concerns than were nonworkers (Berelson, et al., 1954). A study of the recruitment of party workers in California

[12] See the appendix for details of the index.

found that private gain was not an acceptable motivation for party work; presumably some concern with issues and programs was required (Marvick & Nixon, 1961). The survey in Evanston found 86 per cent of party actives, but only 66 per cent of the general citizenry ($p < .05$), agreeing with this statement: "I would like to be active in politics in order to change things for the better" (Jensen, 1960). A nationwide study of party followers and leaders found that party leaders had more elaborately developed conceptions of politics, which also were more extremely liberal or conservative, than their respective followers (McClosky, et al., 1960). A recent study has data challenging this finding: top party leaders were found to be more moderate on issues than lower-level leaders (rejected caucus nominees) (Constantini, 1963).

It seems likely that whether or not party workers are motivated by ideology is affected by the nature of the local party system. Workers in urban political machines are notorious for their lack of concern about issues and their high concern about patronage. In other settings, where the monetary stakes of politics are lower and the party system is more open to widespread recruitment, one would expect ideology and issues to be more important as a motivation.

A curious relationship appears in the research data which probably can be explained by differentials in the sophistication of political concepts and beliefs. Some studies have shown that persons who favor an internationalist (in contrast to isolationist) posture for United States foreign policy are more likely to be active in politics (Campbell, et al., 1960; Connelly & Field, 1944). Both variables probably are a function of sophistication about politics. Internationalists are significantly more sophisticated about politics than isolationists (Campbell, et al., 1960, p. 200). Another tenable hypothesis is that persons with an activist posture toward life would be more likely to become active in politics and also would be more likely to desire an active role for the United States in world affairs. Only additional careful research can disclose whether either of these interpretations accurately explains the phenomena.

What kinds of social and cultural factors are likely to create conceptual sophistication about politics? The five-nation study showed some political-cultural differences between nations in this respect. Respondents were asked to name national leaders of the principal parties and to name cabinet offices or departments. Generally, the Germans, Americans, and British performed better on this simple test of political knowledge than the Italians and Mexicans (Almond & Verba, 1963, p. 96). Americans were most likely to be willing to express opinions on six general political attitudes, followed by British, Germans, Mexicans, and Italians (p. 97). This pattern of differences conforms to the general level of politicization found in the respective national cultures: of the five nations, the United States and the United Kingdom ranked highest on politicization, Germany and Mexico were intermediary, and Italy ranked lowest. Politicization is the amount of interest in, knowledge about, and conceptual sophistication of politics held by a person.

Within nations, too, there are important social-position differences in levels of politicization; these tend to be the same factors that made for high interest, high duty, and high efficacy. **Persons of high SES, especially high education, are more likely to have greater knowledge of and more sophistication about politics than persons of low SES** (Campbell, et al., 1960; Lazarsfeld, et al., 1944; Saenger, 1945). This proposition is almost a truism, since education is designed to increase knowledge and sophistication. Furthermore, persons who are capable of mastering higher education are also more capable of making fine discriminations in their conceptions of politics. The difference is not entirely due to education; other social-position characteristics enter as well. Persons living in environments with more money and higher social status more frequently encounter political persons, objects, and events. They also are more likely to observe greater variation in political phenomena. Increased political sophistication is the natural result of these environmental advantages. Speaking generally, *political sophistication also is a simple function of having lived longer, having had more experience, and having learned more* (Lazarsfeld, et al., 1944).

Conceptual sophistication about politics also has its roots

in personality needs. One scholar has suggested that the pursuit of meaning goes back to a physiological drive (curiosity and/or the need to explore) as well as to early socializing and educational experiences arousing curiosity and interest. The more curious and interested personality becomes more sophisticated politically. In contrast, some persons may cling to ignorance to serve other needs: avoidance of conflict, fear of losing tension-releasing opinions, avoidance of useless effort, avoidance of loss of friends, inability to devote interest and attention to other than private affairs (Lane, 1959, p. 114).

In addition to these simple quantitative measures of knowledge and sophistication, we can look at conceptions of the self and the self-role in politics. These seem to perform placing functions for the individual (Smith, et al., 1956). A person needs to find meaning in his political life (Lane, 1959); he needs to find his own identity in contrast to other political identities. Many persons have a clear and consistent picture of themselves in relation to politics. The first question on an interview schedule used at Northwestern University to study political participation was designed to put the respondent at ease in talking about the topic. He was asked, "In general, do you consider yourself the kind of person who would be likely to be active in politics?" Answers to this item showed a higher correlation (.65) with active participation in politics than any other item in the study (Jensen, 1960). Respondents seemed to have a clear self-image indicating that they were either the political or the nonpolitical type. The most frequent reasons given were lack of interest (or being interested) and that it didn't (or did) fit with their personal inclination. A study in Waukegan, Illinois, found a high correlation between verbal expressions about the certainty of voting and actual voting (M. Miller, 1952). These bits of evidence suggest that a thorough study of self-conceptions of political role very likely would find a high correlation between conceived role and actual participation.

Another type of role conception probably influences political participation, although no evidence can be brought to bear at this time. It was mentioned in Chapter I that some persons conceive of politics as a leisure-time activity, while others conceive of it as part of their work or everyday responsibilities. Obviously, the person who conceives of politics as a professional or occupational responsibility will participate more frequently or consistently. For those who conceive of politics as leisure-time activity, the likelihood of participation will depend a great deal on whether or not they think of politics as fun or satisfying. The person who thinks of politics as leisure and, in addition, dislikes political action almost surely will take no action. On the other hand, the person who thinks of politics as part of his job will take political action whether he likes it or not.

A person's conceptual posture toward politics is embedded in a hierarchy of values. The value placed on political action (rank in the hierarchy) varies considerably from individual to individual. *Persons whose energies are absorbed in personal problems are likely to place little value on participation in politics* (Rosenberg, 1962). *It is easier for a person to allocate energy to politics if the energy demands of the political act are low; as energy demands rise, the frequency of participation declines* (Saenger, 1945). The hierarchy of acts shown in Figure 3, Chapter I, is basically one of energy costs. Psychologically, some persons find the subject matter of politics not compelling (Rosenberg, 1954-1955). In the Evanston survey, 66 per cent of spectators, but only 12 per cent of gladiators ($p < .001$), agreed with this statement: "Other than voting, I just don't have time for politics" (Jensen, 1960). From his study of New Haven, Dahl concluded: "At any given moment, however, only the citizens who expect current decisions to have important and immediate consequences tend to be very active. And they are generally few in number" (1961, p. 297). Most persons anticipate they will receive greater rewards from private (nonpolitical) activities than from political action.

Whether politics is conceived of as unimportant and uninteresting or as important and exciting probably correlates highly with exposure to political information and with psychological involvement in politics, as well as with political action. *Persons who conceive of politics as important — that it deals with great events, great men, and crucial questions —*

TABLE III. 7

General Citizens and Party Actives Compared on Feeling of Importance of Political Participation [a]

Response to question: "Some people feel it is good or important to participate in political affairs. Others feel that it is bad or not important to do so. What is your opinion?"	General Citizenry	Party Actives	Total
Bad or not important	5 (4%)		5 (3%)
Sometimes good or important, sometimes not	56 (44%)	2 (4%)	58 (34%)
Good or important	62 (49%)	44 (96%)	106 (61%)
Don't know	4 (3%)		4 (2%)
Total	127 (100%)	46 (100%)	173 (100%)

[a]Data are from a survey of Evanston citizens and party workers conducted by a Northwestern University graduate seminar (Jensen, 1960).

are more likely to participate in politics (Pesonen, 1961). In the Evanston political participation study, a high relationship was found between feeling politics to be important and participating in politics (see Table III.7) (Jensen, 1960). In this same study, 85 per cent of party actives and 61 per cent of the general citizenry ($p < .01$) agreed with this statement: "I think that being active in politics would be exciting." Eighty-three per cent of actives, but only 42 per cent of general citizens ($p < .001$) agreed with this statement: "I think I would enjoy the challenge of politics." Some recent studies show that a feeling of the importance and mission of serving the public is by far the most important motive attracting federal executives to public service and sustaining their performance on the job (Mann, 1964; Warner, et al., 1963).

Basic conceptions about politics certainly affect the way a person relates to it. Some basic conceptions are whether politics is dirty or clean, open or closed, inefficacious or efficacious for solving problems. These are important correlates of political cynicism, which is discussed in the next section. We know relatively little about why some persons develop negative conceptions of politics and others do not. It certainly seems to be affected by political culture. One study suggests that *persons living in areas dominated by strong political machines are more likely to conceive of politics as dirty and closed than persons living in areas with more open local party systems* (Litt, 1963). Although there are many persons with negative conceptions of politics in the United States, the proportion of such persons is less than in some other countries, notably Italy (Almond & Verba, 1963). A study of businessmen in Philadelphia shows that by and large they seemed to have positive attitudes toward politics and politicians (Janosik, 1962). A study of *nonvoters* in the United States shows they *are less likely to see corruption in politics than voters* (Connelly & Field, 1944). The Evanston survey showed that *spectators were no more likely to feel they would be ridiculed for being active in politics, or that their friends and family would resent it, than were gladiators* (Jensen, 1960). A thorough study of conceptions of politics and how those conceptions arise is needed.

PARTICIPATION AS A FUNCTION OF PERSONALITY

It is not easy to establish clear and reliable connections between personality and political behavior. This problem stems from two kinds of difficulties. First, it is difficult to measure personality: it is not accessible to direct measurement, it can only be inferred from behavior. Such inferences are complicated by lack of clear correspondence between manifestation and personality. Seemingly identical acts by different individuals may spring from different personality needs, and seemingly different acts may spring from the same personality need.

Second, the impact of personality on behavior is mediated through beliefs and attitudes, which also are influenced by cognitions and cognitive learning. The relationship of all these variables, as the author conceives them, can be seen in Figure 4, Chapter I. The "distance" of personality from behavior means that the impact of personality forces on behavior is often more latent than manifest; it may come forth strongly in some situations and have almost no influence in others. Robert Lane, one of the foremost scholars of personality and political behavior, takes this perspective:

> Some situations so clearly structure behavior; some roles leave so little room for personal choice; and some social norms are so unambiguous that personal differences have little effect upon behavior. On the other hand some situations afford considerable "scope" for personality to affect behavior. Among these are the following:
>> Situations where reference groups have politically conflicting points of view.
>> Situations at the focus of conflicting propaganda.
>> Current situations which for any individual are in conflict with previous experience.
>> Situations where social roles are ambiguous, strange, and unfamiliar.
>
> Some types of behavior are less likely to offer scope for the expression of personal differences. These would, by and large, include the more conventional items, such as voting, expressing patriotic opinions, and accepting election results as final, at least temporarily. On the other hand, those types of expression which are more likely to reveal the idiosyncratic features of personality include:
>> Selection of the grounds for rationalizing a political act.
>> Selecting topics for political discussion.
>> Selecting types of political behavior over and above voting.
>> Expression of the probable consequences of participation.
>> Holding particular images of other participants.
>> Styles of personal interaction in political groups (Lane, 1959, pp. 99-100).

Personality is a complicated, interrelated, and interacting system. The study of a complete personality, such as might be carried out by a psychoanalyst, is time-consuming and requires special training. Case studies of this type show rather convincingly how personality affects political behavior (Smith, et al., 1956; Lane, 1962), but the time costs of such studies are so great that it is difficult to get enough cases to arrive at generalizations that one can be confident would hold for the great mass of people. Furthermore, the personality dynamics leading to a political act are so complex as to defy succinct summarization. Consequently, no attempt is made in this book to summarize psychoanalytic or depth studies of personality and political behavior.

Personality also can be studied, in somewhat more piecemeal fashion, by using scales to measure specific personality traits. The methods of trait psychology enable one to administer scales and tests to large numbers of people and to establish statistical relationships between traits and behavior patterns. The discussion to follow depends mainly on the findings of trait psychology. These are uneven in coverage: certain traits have been well investigated, while others are neglected. These findings also are difficult to interpret because of the measurement difficulties mentioned above. Failure to discover a relationship between a trait and behavior may mean that, in fact, there is no relationship, but also it may mean that the researcher's measuring tool does not measure what he hoped it was measuring. If a researcher finds no correlation between a cynicism scale and political activity, it may mean that, in reality, there is no relationship, but it also may mean that either his measure of cynicism or his measure of activity is faulty. Conversely, finding a relationship may not be proof of its existence; relationships can appear as an artifact of measurement bias. The discussion above of the possible biasing effect of response set is germane here. One must question the assumption that a scale measures what the designer intended it to. In this section, syndromes of traits are discussed rather than specific scales. If similar results are discovered when similar, but not identical, scales are administered to different samples, one has increased confidence that a relationship does in fact exist between a trait and political behavior (Campbell & Fiske, 1959).

Sociability

It has been observed many times that politicians are gladhanding extroverts. Does it follow that a sociable personality is a prerequisite for political action? Some scholars believe that man has a social need, and that filling this need is an important motive for engaging in political action (Davies, 1963, pp. 34-36). Sociability is here defined as the possession of social skills and a feeling of ease and graciousness in social relationships. **Sociable personalities are more likely to enter politics than nonsociable personalities; this is especially true of political activities that require social interaction** (Milbrath, 1960a; Milbrath & Klein, 1962; Kuroda, 1964). The studies supporting this point used similar, but not identical, measures of sociability, and the differential effects of socioeconomic status were controlled. Sociable persons were significantly more likely to engage in activities requiring social interaction: campaigning, contacting politicians, soliciting political funds, and being consulted on policy. Behaviors not requiring social interaction, such as being active in a party, contributing money, or attending meetings, had lower correlations (nonsignificant on one sample).

It was necessary to control for SES in these studies because there is a positive correlation between SES and sociability. A correlation between sociability and participation could be a mere artifact of the well-known correlation between SES and political participation. The relationship between sociability and participation, however, was significant even with SES controls. Sociability should be called a necessary but not sufficient condition for entering politics. Many sociable persons do not become active. The reverse is not true, however; a nonsociable person has a barrier to participation in socially interactive political behavior.

The five-nation study gathered information about the general social activity patterns of their respondents, finding cross-national differences in general social activity levels. *Nations that were high on social activity* (the United States and the United Kingdom) *also were high on the level of participation in politics by their citizenry* (Almond & Verba, 1963, Ch. 10). Nations low on social and political activity (especially Italy) had a relatively high percentage of persons who did not feel confident and safe in interacting with other persons.

A study of opinion leaders found that gregariousness

was related to public affairs opinion leadership (Katz & Lazarsfeld, 1955). Some scholars have suggested that while the possession of social skills facilitates entry into politics, overly high social aspirations could lead a person away from politics toward more immediately gratifying social activities (Rosenberg, 1954-1955; also Lane, 1959). One study found no correlation between gregariousness and political activity (Hennessy, 1959).

Another trait that probably belongs in the same syndrome with sociability is a sense of personal esteem; the two are highly intercorrelated (Milbrath & Klein, 1962). It is difficult for a person who does not have a reasonably high estimation of his personal worth to interact naturally with other persons. *People who like themselves and who expect most others to like them find it easier to enter the political fray* (Milbrath & Klein, 1962). *Such persons tend to have more "faith in people" and in politicians, which facilitates their participation in politics* (Lane, 1959; Rosenberg, 1956). Those nations which were low on social and political activity especially seemed to have many persons with very low faith in people; the latter trait, in turn, was related to political trust (Almond & Verba, 1963, Ch. 10).

Ego Strength

Other terms that might apply to this syndrome are self-confidence, sense of competence, or sense of effectiveness. Traits in this syndrome are positively correlated with sociability and esteem; apparently, many of the same environmental conditions that create sociability also create ego strength. The personal effectiveness scale, discussed above under attitudes, is one example of a scale that measures this trait. The reader will recall that it correlated positively with political efficacy and also that persons who feel personally effective are more likely to become active in politics.

The statistically demonstrated relationship between personal effectiveness and political participation (see Table III.3) corresponds with some earlier speculations. One scholar characterized the "autonomous character" as a person with high competence and with high affect toward politics; such a person would be more likely to be active in politics (Riesman, 1952). Another speculated that persons with a desire to be creative and those with a need for ego enhancement would be inclined to become active in politics (Rosenberg, 1951).

As might be expected, *persons growing up in an upper-middle or upper SES environment are more likely to develop self-confidence and feelings of competence than those from a lower SES environment. This is especially characteristic of persons who achieve the higher ranks of education* (Campbell, et al., 1960; Dahl, 1961). The reader is reminded of Dahl's argument, discussed earlier, that environment and feelings of confidence and efficacy have interactive effects on one another. Dahl found that if the effects of feelings of confidence and efficacy were controlled statistically, the relationship between SES and political participation was no longer statistically significant (1961, pp. 291-292). This suggests that environment primarily affects political participation through shaping personality traits like sociability and ego strength.

It is also difficult to separate the effects of environment from those of heredity in developing feelings of confidence and effectiveness. The more generously endowed child, who is sensitive and analytical, learns to manipulate successfully the objects and persons in his environment early in life. If he is also well coordinated and successful athletically, his sense of mastery will be enhanced. The rewards of successful manipulation soon build a firm personality trait of self-confidence. A child of this type who also lives in a high SES environment is given many opportunities to encounter and master different types of situations; consequently, he has little fear of social, business, or political challenge. His low SES counterpart, who may be equally gifted, will have less broad familiarity with challenging situations.

One additional bit of evidence bears on this trait. One study found that *persons who score highly on the personal effectiveness scale are less likely to resent government*

(Stokes, 1962). One can speculate that persons who feel effective in dealing with their environment also feel effective in dealing with government and, thus, are less inclined to resent government or to feel that it does not respond to their efforts.

Anomie, Alienation, Cynicism

This syndrome of traits is, in a sense, the opposite of sociability and competence. *Persons who score highly on anomie, alienation, and cynicism are less likely to become active in politics.* Such persons not only hesitate to take gladiatorial action, but they are likely to withdraw from spectator action as well. Although these three traits are related, they are sufficiently distinct that each is discussed in turn.

The term "anomie," or "anomia," as it is sometimes called, originated with Durkheim and has been used by many other social scientists. Anomic persons exhibit a lack of values and lack of direction; they feel ineffective; they tend to believe that authority figures do not care about them; activity loses its point and its urgency.[13] A short anomie scale, developed by Srole, has been used in many studies (Meier & Bell, 1959; Srole, 1951; Srole, 1956).

John Schaar developed an "anomie" scale from some of the personality items (two from the efficacy scale and two from the personal effectiveness scale) included in the Survey Research Center 1956 study of the national electorate;[14] the four items were scaled by Guttman (1949) techniques. This scale was cross-tabulated with the Campaign Activity Index (CAI) and with all six specific acts included in the index. In each instance, anomie was negatively correlated with participation; highly anomic persons were less likely to become active in politics. The correlation with the CAI was significant, even though statistical controls for response set, for interest in the election, and for concern about the outcome of the election were applied. A control for education did bring the size of the correlation between anomie and participation below

---

[13]See Lane (1959, pp. 166-169) for a review of the origin and meaning of anomie as a concept and of the findings relating it to political participation.

[14]See the appendix for the items.

the level of significance. This suggests that educational achievement is an important counteraction to anomie. Another study shows anomie correlating more highly with education than any other variable in the study (Meier, 1963).

Scholars have speculated freely on the relation of anomie to participation in politics. One has thought that feelings of being alone and weak and also feelings of fatalism would tend to make a person apathetic politically (Rosenberg, 1951; Rosenberg, 1954-1955). Another suggested that persons with ineffective engagement of their egos are unlikely to participate (Allport, 1945). Others have speculated that persons with a relatively high level of personal anxiety use all of their psychic energy for that concern and are unlikely to divert energy to political activity (Goldhamer, 1950; Lane, 1959; Mussen & Wyszinski, 1952; Rosenberg, 1962).

Alienation and cynicism imply a more active rejection of politics than the passive withdrawal or detachment of anomie. Campbell has made this distinction:

> The detached person may simply never have learned to communicate at the community level or the physical circumstances of his life may make communication difficult. He lives within a restricted life space without much sense of restriction and without great affect toward the outside world. Our surveys show us, however, that there is a different kind of individual whose orientation toward the world of politics is not simply one of detachment, but of suspicion, distrust, hostility, and cynicism. These people believe that political office holders are corrupt, self-seeking and incompetent, that the whole political process is a fraud and a betrayal of the public trust (Campbell, 1962, p. 14).

Several recent studies have found that **persons who feel cynical about or alienated from politics are much less likely to participate in politics** (Agger, et al., 1961; Almond & Verba, 1963; Campbell, 1962; Erbe, 1964; Janda, 1965; Kornhauser, et al., 1956; Kuroda, 1964; Levin, 1960; Litt, 1963; McDill & Ridley, 1962; Rosenberg, 1954-1955; Stokes, 1962; Thompson & Horton, 1960). This general attitude seems to have several dimensions. Preliminary evidence from a study shows that misanthropes (those with low "faith in people") have little faith in the qualifications of voters, in the responsiveness of legislators, or in the integrity of candidates, fear unrestricted freedom of speech, and are willing to see the state used as an instrument of suppression (Rosenberg, 1956).

It is important for the health of political society to understand how cynicism and alienation are developed as personality traits. The environment in which a person is raised has an important impact. Several studies show that **persons of higher SES, especially higher education, are less likely to develop cynical attitudes toward politics** (Agger, et al., 1961; Almond & Verba, 1963; Erbe, 1964; Kornhauser, et al., 1956). This finding is disputed by two other studies which found no correlation between cynicism and education (Campbell, 1962; Litt, 1963). Another set of studies suggest that *persons living in communities with urban political machines are more likely to develop cynical attitudes toward politics. The longer the residence in the machine-dominated city, the greater the cynicism* (Levin, 1960; Litt, 1963).[15]

The five-nation study showed differences in alienation from politics across national political cultures. The highest percentage of alienated persons was found in Italy and Mexico; Great Britain and Germany were at an intermediate level; and the lowest percentage was in the United States (Almond & Verba, 1963, p. 99). Political alienation seemed to be related to general attitudes of social trust and distrust; *those who had faith in people tended also to exhibit politically relevant trust* (p. 285). Persons living in Great Britain and the United States were most likely to have attitudes of social trust, Germans were next most likely, while the Italians and Mexicans were most likely to exhibit attitudes of social distrust (p. 267). The close correspondence between attitudes of social trust and political trust most clearly held in the United States and the United Kingdom; in the other three nations there was less fusion between social and political attitudes (p. 287).

[15]Agger, et al. (1964) have speculated along the same lines.

Another study shows that *persons who are involved in social organizations are less likely to feel alienated from society and politics.* In fact, Erbe (1964), using a second-order partialling operation, found no correlation between alienation and political participation with SES and involvement in nonpolitical organizations held constant. This finding should not be interpreted to mean that alienation does not affect participation in politics; it could mean simply that environmental factors like SES and organizational participation are important in developing alienated or nonalienated personalities. Some studies show that *older persons are more likely to feel cynical and alienated from politics than younger persons* (Agger, et al., 1961; Kornhauser, et al., 1956). The correlation was not just an artifact of the trend for younger persons to obtain more education than their elders. The researchers found that the poorly educated were more cynical even with age controlled, and the elderly were more cynical even with education controlled. This finding is not contradictory to that reported elsewhere that older persons are more interested in politics and more likely to vote than younger persons. The correlations are not perfect; not all older persons are interested in politics and not all are cynical. Although it is unlikely that the same person would be interested in and cynical about politics, it still is possible for older persons to rank higher than younger on both variables.

Dominance, Manipulativeness

It is often supposed that individuals with a personal need for status and power over others naturally gravitate to politics to fulfill their craving. Hobbes and Nietzsche built their political philosophies around this central assumption. In his early writings, notably *Psychopathology and Politics*, Harold Lasswell set forth his famous formula for the developmental sequence of political man. Restating the symbolism of his formula into verbal terms, he said that the private motives, which had been nurtured in the person's early life in the family (especially the motive for power), might become displaced onto public objects. These displaced private motives would tend to be rationalized in terms of the public interest and, thus, ordinary man became transformed into political man. Later Lasswell qualified his position, suggesting that power is a nonprimary motive; considering it the sole or major motive for entering politics was too inflexible an explanation. He thought it more likely that political leaders would seek such values as respect, rectitude, and wealth. If a person did enter politics only to seek power, he would be likely to be restrained by other political actors and might not rise above a lesser position (Lasswell, 1954).[16]

The available empirical evidence on this point (for the United States only) suggests that *persons with high power motivation are not likely to enter politics* (other arenas, such as business or the military, provide better opportunities to dominate others), *and if they do, they are not likely to be very successful at it.*[17] A dominance scale was administered in three studies of political participation (Milbrath, 1960b; Milbrath & Klein, 1962; Jensen, 1960). Only a slight trend appeared for dominants to be more likely to become active in politics, and in only one study was the relationship statistically significant, and that just barely. A study of South Carolina legislators found them only slightly more dominant than a sample from the general population (McConaughy, 1950). A study of office-holders found no correlation between power motive and holding public office (Browning & Jacob, 1964). When only offices with high power or with a clear road to success were considered, the correlation was significant. The researchers also found a correlation between achievement motive and holding public office in political systems where the office had high achievement potential. In sum, the evidence suggests that a desire for dominance and power provides only a weak attraction toward general political action; only in special cases affording clear use of power (rare in politics) could power be considered a significant or primary motivation.

If additional evidence should confirm that power-hungry

---

[16]Jacob (1962) and Rosenzweig (1957) have also suggested that respect is a high motive for entering politics.

[17]Lane (1959, pp. 124-128) has an excellent discussion of the belief that political man seeks power and suggests why this supposed relationship is not borne out by the evidence.

persons are not particularly likely to go into politics, how would one explain the lack of relationship? It is quite likely that a certain proportion of any population does develop strong motives for power and that some, but not many, do find their way into politics. A very strong power motive may be the outward manifestation of a deep need for reassurance and a cover for feelings of unworthiness and low self-esteem. We saw above that persons of low ego strength are not likely to enter politics. The person who attaches great importance to imposing his will on others is not likely to be very successful in democratic politics; he may alienate instead of attract followers. He may be unwilling to take orders or to serve menially as a way of working his way up in a political party.

Another factor is that the political arena is not a particularly fruitful place to find fulfillment for power needs; there is too little opportunity for direct satisfaction. The worlds of finance, industry, or the military may be more satisfying to a man with lust for power. For many people, the need for power is most visibly satisfied in primary relationships. Perhaps it is enough for such persons that they can be autocrats in their own homes. There are, then, many other environments, in addition to politics, where the need for power can be satisfied; many of them carry fewer uncertainties than politics.

The desire to manipulate is somewhat different from the desire for power. One study found politicals more willing to compromise than apoliticals (Hennessy, 1959). Another found law students planning to go into politics scoring higher on a manipulative scale than those not planning to enter politics (Agger, 1956a). There is no evidence that political actives necessarily have a desire or need to manipulate, but the willingness to manipulate and the ability to be successful at it probably facilitates entry into politics.

Authoritarianism

Revulsion from Nazi-Fascist experience before and during World War II has stimulated a great number of studies of authoritarianism[18] and has added a popular word to our vocabulary. All sorts of behaviors and persons are character-

[18] A landmark study was Adorno, et al. (1950).

ized as authoritarian, and this wide usage makes definition of the trait extremely difficult and somewhat arbitrary. An operational definition has not been agreed upon by the academic profession, either. There does seem to be consensus that authoritarians like to issue orders and receive complete and unquestioning obedience. They also tend to be submissive to and unquestioning of persons with authority over them. Other qualities have been added to the definition by various scholars, but nearly all of them are disputed by other scholars.

Despite the rash of studies,[19] there is relatively little reliable evidence in the form of substantiated propositions about the impact of authoritarianism on political behavior. Part of the failure stems from inadequate operational definitions and other methodological difficulties. In the early versions of the Fascism (*F*) scale (the most widely used measure of authoritarianism, developed by Adorno, et al., 1950), all the items were scored positively and were heavily subject to response-set bias. Once this was discovered, new versions, with half the items worded so that they would be scored negatively, were developed.[20] But even the new versions seldom showed a relationship to political behavior. Few attempts at scaling the items by Guttman (1949) techniques have been successful, suggesting that the items make up a syndrome rather than a single trait. After all these years of research, one is still required to say that the concept is not satisfactorily operationalized, no clear and precise definition of the trait (if it is one) can be given, and evidence about the relationship of the concept to political behavior is highly inconclusive.

Because of these factors, a review of the following findings relating authoritarianism to political participation should be taken with a grain of salt and with a wait-and-see attitude. The findings are interesting, even if they are not conclusive. Those relating authoritarianism to direction of political behavior (which are not reviewed here) are even more exten-

---

[19] See Christie & Cook (1958) for a compilation of references to that date.
[20] The new version of Christie and his associates (1958) was one of the more successful.

sive than those relevant to political action, but they are no more conclusive. It is not known if authoritarians are more likely to vote Democratic or Republican, to be liberal or conservative, to support extremist politics or not.

Christie's version of the F scale with half its items reversed (Christie, et al., 1958) was included in the Survey Research Center's nationwide study of the American electorate in 1956 and, therefore, could be cross-tabulated with the Campaign Activity Index. It showed no significant relationship to that index or to any of the specific political activities incorporated in it. Statistical controls for response set and for education did not succeed in bringing out a relationship. Two other studies found no relationship between authoritarianism and participation in politics (Harned, 1961; Hennessy, 1959).

In contrast, certain other studies show high authoritarians as disinclined to participate in politics. One reported high authoritarians scoring low on efficacy and being less likely to vote (Janowitz & Marvick, 1953). Another found no correlation between authoritarianism and likelihood of voting, but found a slight tendency for authoritarians to be less likely to campaign, to have a lower level of political interest, and to score lower on efficacy (Lane, 1955). A third study found high authoritarians less likely to join groups (we have already seen that group activity and political activity go together) and less likely to participate in politics. Unfortunately, this study used no SES or response-set controls, yet the early version of the F scale used is strongly biased by both factors (Sanford, 1950).

A study of factory workers showed that high authoritarians are more likely to be dissatisfied with life (Kornhauser, et al., 1956). The discussion above indicated that alienated, cynical, and anomic persons were disinclined to participate; the same may hold true for dissatisfied persons. Another study found that highly authoritarian lobbyists were significantly less likely than less authoritarian lobbyists to participate in several specific political acts. The F scale[21] separated party actives from nonactives better ($p < .001$) than any other

[21] The same Christie version used in the SRC 1956 election study

variable in the study (Milbrath, 1960a; Milbrath & Klein, 1962). All of the respondents in the study were upper-middle or upper class, and all had the same occupation. Statistical controls were used to guard against the occurrence of response-set bias.

If additional data should confirm that high authoritarians are not likely to participate in politics, how could this be explained? Authoritarians, according to the theory, prefer an environment where status relationships are clear and stable, where it is accepted that one follows orders from above and receives obedience from those below. This kind of environment is much less likely to be found in politics than in some other environments, such as a corporate bureaucracy. The political world often is unstructured and ambiguous. This is especially characteristic of United States politics, which is much less structured by political parties than is true of many other societies. Persons who have a low tolerance for ambiguity are likely to be uncomfortable in politics, and it has generally been found that authoritarians have a low tolerance for ambiguity.

Politics often presents a situation in which one person is trying to convince another that he should do a certain thing; compliance usually is obtained by persuasion and not by the application of sanctions. Because of their personality, authoritarians tend not to be skillful or at ease in this type of social interaction. One study found a significant negative correlation between sociability and the F scale (Milbrath & Klein, 1962). All of the above factors suggest why authoritarians might be uncomfortable in democratic politics. Whether they would be attracted to extremist politics (many such movements have rigid leader-follower relationships) is difficult to say; there is no statistical evidence either way.

Intellectuality

Intellectuality as a personality trait is somewhat different from intellectual ability as measured by intelligence tests, although the two may be correlated. Intellectuality is a posture of seeking full information and reasoning one's way to a conclusion. It implies an intellectual standard for the quality of evidence one must have before he believes something.

Relatively little work has been done with this trait, and there is no widely accepted scale for measuring it. One scholar has hypothesized that intellectually lazy persons would not be likely to enter politics (Rosenberg, 1954-1955). A study of nonvoters showed them to be less tolerant of conflict and more accepting of the *status quo* (less inclined to search for new and better arrangements) than voters (Connelly & Field, 1944).

A study of lobbyists found that those who scored low on intellectuality were significantly less likely to be active in a party, to feel strongly about their party identification, to participate in political campaigns, and to have held a public office at some point in their careers (Milbrath, 1960a). Another study showed a significant positive correlation (.54) between a rating for astuteness and participation in politics (Milbrath, 1956). A study in Finland showed that persons who tended to be passive cognitively were more likely to take an extremist orientation to politics (Pesonen, 1961). These findings are too scattered to provide confidence about generalizations relating intellectuality to political participation; much more research with this trait is needed. One might expect intellectuality to correlate positively with sociability, personal effectiveness, and education (all of which are positively correlated with political participation). Thus, a multiple correlational or partialling procedure should be used to ascertain whether or not intellectuality makes an independent contribution to political participation.

Expressive-Instrumental

In Chapter I, an expressive-instrumental distinction was made between the motivations leading to political acts: expressive acts are immediately drive-reducing to the actor, while instrumental acts lead through a chain of action to a final goal. Personalities inclined expressively (having strong expressive needs) tend to take political actions emphasizing expressive rewards, whereas personalities enjoying manipulation tend to take instrumental action. One scholar has suggested that personalities not extremely expressive or extremely instrumental, who have both motivations for their action, would be likely to make the best citizens in a democracy (Himmelstrand, 1960a; Himmelstrand, 1960b). A study in India suggested that certain Indian intellectuals take an expressive role toward politics. These persons generally do not have power and responsibility in the regime, entering politics only when a great deal is at stake or when a crisis requires action in support of an ideal. Decrying patronage and personal political rewards, they serve without pay and function without elaborate party machinery, devotion to the ideal being their sole reward (Shils, 1961).

Despite these intriguing speculations about the relation of expressives and instrumentalists to the political process, there is little reliable statistical evidence to back them up. We don't know the likelihood of each type taking political action, and we don't know the environmental conditions which encourage or facilitate action by each type. As improved tools for measurement are developed and statistical data are gathered,[22] the sharpening of concepts and the security of findings should improve. Until then, we must be content with intriguing speculations.

Conclusions

The role of personality in attracting people to politics or keeping them out of politics probably is much more pervasive than the sketchy research evidence presented here can indicate. The available evidence suggests that persons` with great neurotic or psychotic problems are not attracted to normal democratic political action. The chaotic, rough-and-tumble environment of competitive politics carries few rewards for thin-skinned, neurotic personalities. Such persons might be attracted to extremist politics under certain conditions, but there are no data specifying such conditions. This is not to say that political actives do not have neurotic needs — probably many of them do — but they usually have their impulses under control and clothe their motives with the garb of public interest. Their defense mechanisms are strong enough to withstand political shock and disappointment. A finding from the Evanston survey, cited earlier, is relevant here: 83 per cent of the party actives said they

[22] Himmelstrand has taken a lead here.

"enjoyed the challenge of politics," but only 42 per cent of the cross-section of citizens thought they would enjoy it.

The data suggest that political gladiators are persons who are particularly well equipped to deal with their environment. They feel personally competent; they know themselves and feel confident of their knowledge and skills; their ego is strong enough to withstand blows; they are not burdened by a load of anxiety and internal conflict; they can control their impulses; they are astute, sociable, self-expressive, and responsible. Although they may desire to dominate and manipulate others, political gladiators do not seem to lean any further in this direction than persons in many other roles. Gladiators seem to glory in political battle and are self-sufficient enough to withstand the rough-and-tumble of partisan politics. The political arena is not a hospitable place for insecure, timid, and withdrawn people who do not have great faith in their ability to deal effectively with their environment.

IV

POLITICAL PARTICIPATION AS A
FUNCTION OF POLITICAL SETTING

IN THIS CHAPTER we move one step farther back in the conceptual diagram (Figure 4, Chapter I) to environment, focusing especially on the political setting part of the environment, which defines, channels, and confines the political participation of individuals living in that setting. Political setting is defined here as composed of the following three factors: (1) rules of the game about the conduct of politics; (2) political institutions, especially the political party system; (3) the special characteristics of a given campaign. These three kinds of factors cannot be neatly distinguished in analysis. Rules of the game, for example, cannot be separated from institutions, and institutions, in turn, organize activities in specific campaigns. The three factors can serve as general topics around which discussion can be organized, however.

Political setting can be looked at somewhat more broadly, too, as an entire national political culture. The five-nation study, as well as many others, has demonstrated that patterns and rates of political participation differ from nation to nation. Participation rates were generally found to be higher in the United States and the United Kingdom than in Germany and Mexico and were especially low in Italy (Almond & Verba, 1963). Tracing the origins of these differences is very difficult. To a certain extent, they may be traceable to differences in political forms and traditions. However, some of them may also stem from social conditions such as child-rearing practices, levels of education, class barriers, and so forth. For example, when persons of equal educational attainment in different countries are compared, cross-national differences in rates of participation are substantially reduced (Almond & Verba, 1963, p. 338). Careful studies in many nations will be required before the multiple factors causing national cultural differences in participation can be properly assessed. Purely physical factors such as terrain, distance, and weather are not political, but they, too, affect participation. The person who has to climb over a mountain, or travel a long distance, or go out in inclement weather has a greater energy and time cost for his participation than does a person without such barriers. A higher degree of positive attraction to participate must be present to overcome them. In certain settings, the cost of overcoming these barriers is approximately equal for each citizen and need not be considered in trying to explain individual differences in behavior. When the costs of surmounting physical barriers are unequal from individual to individual, they must be taken into account in the explanation of behavior differences.

RULES OF THE GAME

Eligibility rules are the primary consideration of this section. These have their strongest impact on the likelihood of voting, but they have some influence on participation in gladiatorial activities as well. Persons not eligible to vote in a society are not likely to engage in other political activities either. Mere eligibility, on the other hand, by no means guarantees participation.

Although "universal suffrage" is a common phrase, no society grants total universal suffrage. Children are excluded from voting in every society. Criminals and persons who are physically and mentally incapable usually are excluded. Some scholars estimate that 3 per cent of American adults are excluded from the electorate because of capability rules (Campbell, et al., 1960). Even today, there are many societies where persons are not allowed to vote because they are propertyless, are illiterate, are of the female sex, and so forth.

The struggle for the extension of the suffrage is a fascinating chapter in history.[1] Most of this development occurred

---

[1] See Lane (1959) and Rokkan (1962b) for a more detailed summary of that history.

after the American and French revolutions and went on simultaneously, with variations in pace, in many Western countries. Although there may have been pressure from the disfranchised to be given the vote, in many cases a more important factor was the expectation by a ruling faction that extension of the suffrage would help insure the maintenance of its position in power (Rokkan, 1962b). The impact on the political system of an extension of the suffrage generally was gradual and delayed rather than immediate. The percentage of the newly enfranchised participating in politics tended to rise very gradually with succeeding elections because, in most cases, the new eligibles were mobilized after, rather than before, extension of the suffrage (Rokkan & Valen, 1962; Tingsten, 1937). Since the newly enfranchised generally were less politicized than those eligible at an earlier date, *as suffrage expanded, the total number of participants rose, but the percentage of eligibles participating declined* (Kyogoku & Ike, 1959).

The secret ballot was introduced in many nations in the nineteenth century. The campaign for ballot secrecy was partly justified on the ground that voters needed to be protected from pressure by their superiors. It was also justified by the belief that vote-buying would drop off because there would be no way to be certain of delivery of the vote. However, another, and largely unintended, consequence of the secret ballot was that it protected a voter from pressure by his peers. His work mates, his friends, and perhaps even his family need not know how he voted, if indeed he voted at all, unless he chose to reveal it. The secret vote could be an irresponsible vote, in that the act is separated from the role; normal role sanctions, such as ostracism, rebuke, and so forth, are difficult to apply. Although one might suspect that the separation of the act from role constraints, by the secret ballot, could have important consequences for the functioning of the political system, there is insufficient research on this to be able to say what those consequences are.

Even though suffrage may be "universal," there often are other legal barriers to participation, the most significant being residence requirements. Nearly all political units require new citizens to live a certain length of time in a new residence before they are allowed to vote. A study in 1956 found that most states in the United States require new residents to live two years in the state (two-thirds of the states) and 30 days in the precinct before they are allowed to vote (Goldman, 1956). Only twelve states have residence requirements of less than one year (President's Commission, 1963). Fifteen states now allow new residents to vote for national candidates (President and Vice-President) even if they do not meet the full-term requirements for state and local candidates; seven states also allow presidential voting to former residents (President's Commission, 1963).

Obviously, the more mobile the population, the greater the barrier to participation residence requirements become. The United States Bureau of the Census revealed that 20 million American adults changed residence in 1961. The President's Commission on Registration and Voting Participation (1963) estimated that 4 million persons were disfranchised by residence requirements in 1950, 5 million in 1954, and 8 million in 1960. The author took 1960 census data and ranked states by the percentage of their citizens who changed residence after 1958; this ranking showed a negative correlation ($-.515$) with turnout rankings of the states for the 1960 presidential election: the more mobile the population, the lower the percentage turnout.

An official list of eligible voters can be maintained administratively so as to facilitate as well as to hinder voting. Many countries, and a few localities in the United States, have what is called official or automatic registration. In this system, no initiative by the potential voter is required to get his name on the list of eligibles; the responsibility for keeping the list up to date is with the registration officials. Such a system tends to shift party competition away from the attempt to get partisan supporters to register. If the system is properly administered, not only is it more likely to insure that nearly all eligibles are on the list, but it more certainly sees that persons who died or moved away are removed from the list. Keeping voter registration accurate and up to date naturally is harder in areas of high population mobility. Perhaps a completely automatic system could be utilized only where there is compulsory registration of residence with the police. Some studies have shown that the *percentage turnout for voting is higher under automatic registration* (Gosnell, 1930; Rokkan, 1962b).

Certain states in the United States use a registration system akin to automatic registration. Idaho selects and pays a deputy registrar in each precinct to canvass from door to door and keep registration rolls up to date; Idaho is also a top-ranking state in voting turnout. California law authorizes the appointment of deputy registrars and door-to-door canvassing (President's Commission, 1963). Canada uses teams of enumerators, two to each electoral district, to canvass each residence before each parliamentary election (President's Commission, 1963). In most localities in the United States, however, the act of registration is much more inconvenient than the act of voting. Some states require a trip to the county courthouse, usually during working hours. It helps somewhat if the state makes provision for precinct or mobile registration on designated days preceding elections (over half of the states do so); the voter then makes only a short trip in his immediate neighborhood.

In some states, mainly in the South, registration is more than inconvenient, it is downright difficult. Registration forms are deliberately made complicated. Some jurisdictions require witnesses to testify to the identity and residence of the applicant. Literacy tests in many jurisdictions are extremely difficult and lend themselves to discriminatory abuse. If the registration officials (usually white) are bent on excluding a certain group of potential voters (usually Negro), they can demand letter-perfect accuracy before the registration is accepted. One study found a lower than normal percentage of Negro registrants in counties where literacy tests were difficult or arbitrarily administered (Matthews & Prothro, 1963b). Another study showed the lowest Negro registration in those Louisiana parishes (counties) which had a high percentage of Negroes and in which there was an effort to preserve a plantation economy (Fenton & Vines, 1957).

Most states permit some type of permanent registration so that the citizen does not need to reregister before each election. One scholar has concluded that there was an average difference in turnout of 9 per cent between cities with permanent registration and cities requiring registration before each election (Lane, 1959). Probably many persons who otherwise might have voted on election day do not do so because they had not been foresighted enough to register.

In the not-too-distant past in the United States, the poll tax was another type of barrier thrown in the path of poor people and Negroes who might wish to vote. Persons who could not afford to pay the tax or who overlooked paying it were not allowed to vote on election day. A recent amendment to the United States Constitution forbids the poll tax in federal elections, and it is falling into disuse in state and local elections. A scholar of southern politics estimated that removal of the poll tax would increase voting percentages by only 5 to 10 per cent (Key, 1949).

Certain other legal arrangements also may facilitate voting. Voting procedures standardized from locality to locality and from election to election help remove the fear of "not knowing how." *Short ballots reduce the burden of attempting to become informed and thus facilitate turnout* (Gosnell, 1930; Rokkan, 1962b). Even a highly educated and informed citizen may feel poorly prepared when confronted by a ballot with fifty or more candidates. Certain localities have elections so frequently that voters find it difficult to maintain interest; less frequent elections probably would increase the percentage turning out for elections for more important offices (Lane, 1959). Compulsory voting has been tried at one time or another in several countries, including Belgium, Holland, Switzerland, and Austria, and it does seem to increase turnout. One study concluded that *compulsory voting tended to bring less qualified persons to the polls and increased the percentage of invalid ballots* (Tingsten, 1937). The practice has not spread widely, and some countries have abandoned it.

THE PARTY SYSTEM

Political parties were invented, among other reasons, to help citizens interpret political information and events and to organize and channel their political participation. The political party system inevitably affects patterns and rates of participation in politics. In some localities, there is vigorous party competition, but in other localities the majority party may win so consistently and easily that minor party supporters do not contest very vigorously. Although it is necessary to be cautious about application of the rule to specific situations, it is generally true that **the more competitive the parties, the greater the likelihood of high rates of participation.** A rank ordering of the states on party competition correlated .807 with a ranking of the states on turnout in gubernatorial and senatorial elections from 1952 through 1960 (Milbrath, 1965). A study of four cities in the United States shows that competition between elites (party competition) stimulates mass participation, especially if the competition is ideological (Agger, et al., 1964). A study in the South (where the Democratic party dominates state and local elections) reports that bifactional rivalry within the Democratic party tends to be correlated with increased Negro registration when one or more of the candidates seem favorable to Negroes; contested primaries also tended to stimulate turnout (Matthews & Prothro, 1963b). In Finland, a strong challenge from the Communist party in a constituency tends to increase turnout (Allardt & Bruun, 1956). Nonpartisan elections do not necessarily depress turnout if there is some competition for offices. Turnout in primaries generally is lower than in general elections, but primary turnout tends to be higher where party competition is greater (Lane, 1959).

Party competition probably affects participation by stimulating interest in a campaign and giving citizens the impression that their individual efforts affect the outcome. If party competition does not produce greater interest and a greater sense of efficacy, it probably has little impact on participation.

The competitiveness of parties also affects the activities and roles of political gladiators. A safe major party has no problem recruiting candidates because it is the major, or only, channel to political office; its minor party opponent may have to conscript candidates to run (Seligman, 1961; Standing & Robinson, 1958). Competitive party localities seem to be as likely to develop party factions as safe party localities (Seligman, 1961). Bifactional rather than multi-factional rivalry tends to occur in states with one major party, but where there is also some opposition from a minor party (Key, 1949). Factions in competitive parties tend to be vigorous in recruiting and supporting candidates. There seems to be little central control of candidate recruitment in competitive parties (Seligman, 1961). Improved theorizing and additional research are needed in order to know the applicability and limitations of these generalizations.

The presence or absence of party conflict can affect the relationship of other variables to political participation. We note several places in this book that persons of higher education are more likely to participate in politics. A study in Norway, however, found no relationship between amount of education and participation in politics. This led to the speculation that *the relationship between education and political participation is more marked where the politics of the area play down class differences* (Rokkan, 1962b). The explanation for this requires a brief description of the Norwegian party system. Norway has six political parties, and the party divisions follow socioeconomic cleavages more closely than in the United States. There is a labor party, a farmer's party, a party mainly supported by white-collar persons, and a conservative party supported by business. The Norwegian parties might be called "status-polarized parties," whereas those in the United States might be called "heterogeneous," since many persons from all statuses are found in each party. The leadership of a low-status party, such as the Norwegian labor party, must recruit and train less educated workers to participate in politics; it does not have a readymade educated elite to call on. Thus, the correlation of education with participation in a status-polarized party system tends to be low. Education becomes a more significant variable determining participation in a setting with heterogeneous parties which play down instead of accentuate class differences.

An unusual finding from the Norwegian election studies is that *turnout is higher where the socioeconomic status of an area is more homogeneous* (Rokkan, 1962b; Rokkan & Campbell, 1960). The proposition does not seem to hold for nonpartisan local elections, only for elections where there is some competition between status-polarized parties in a proportional representation system. The interpretation is not so certain as the finding. One can surmise that persons living in homogeneous communities are subjected to fewer cross-pressures. Most of the people around them believe and vote the same way, and they are swept along with the crowd. We know from other studies that *indecision resulting from cross-pressures leads certain persons not to vote at all* (Berelson, et al., 1954; Lazarsfeld, et al., 1944). (A cross-pressured person is one who belongs to two or more groups pulling him in different directions.) Peripheral areas in Norway (those with low population density and difficult geographical access) have fewer party organizations and lower turnout than the more urban and central areas (Rokkan & Valen, 1962).

It has generally been found that turnout at elections in western Europe is higher than turnout in the United States. Some scholars have attempted to trace this to differences in the system of representation. Many western European countries have proportional representation, whereby each party receives seats in the national legislature according to its ratio of the popular vote. Most areas in the United States use a system of single-member districts in which the candidate who obtains a plurality of the vote wins the seat.

Does proportional representation tend to produce higher turnout than the plurality system? The evidence is inconclusive. A study of turnout figures from several countries disclosed that in some countries that switched from the plurality to the proportional representation system turnout increased; the electorate in these countries was maturing simultaneously, however (women were given the vote at about the same time) (Tingsten, 1937). Tingsten concluded that a single-member district system, where one party was dominant, would be likely to have lower turnout (p. 223). New York City tried the proportional representation system for ten years, but it made little difference in turnout (Zeller & Bone, 1948). Turnout was found to be higher for proportional representation than plurality elections in Norway, but the plurality elections also were nonpartisan and generally held in rural areas (both of the latter are correlated with lower turnout) (Rokkan & Valen, 1962). This pattern of evidence leads one to suspect that political interest is the major intervening variable. If the system of representation and election contesting stirs up interest in the populace, they will turn out to vote. If there is little difference between the parties, or if one party is sure to win, the people are likely to be bored and stay at home.

Only a few studies have used strength of party organization as a variable (Cutright, 1963; Cutright & Rossi, 1958; Eldersveld, 1964; Katz & Eldersveld, 1961; Rossi & Cutright, 1961; Wolfinger, 1963). Those that did concentrated more on the effect of strength of party on turning the vote in its direction rather than on the effect of party in getting out the vote. One study found that an increase in minor party activities increased turnout for that party (Katz & Eldersveld, 1961). No correlation was found between strength of party organization and level of political knowledge; party seemed to be less important as a formative influence on opinions than the mass media. There was, however, a greater ideological difference between party supporters in areas of strong party organizations. There is a hint here that strong party organizations would be likely to stimulate participation, but the proposition has not been tested explicitly.

PERSONAL CONTACT

One of the most important stimulants to political participation is personal contact by a party worker; if that worker is also a friend, the contact is even more impressive. It has been found repeatedly that **persons contacted by party workers are more likely to vote and also to participate in gladiatorial activities** (Berelson, et al., 1954; Campbell, et al., 1960; Janowitz & Marvick, 1956; Kitt & Gleicher, 1950; McPhee & Glaser, 1962; Milne & Mackenzie, 1954; Wolfinger, 1963). This relationship is shown in Table IV.1, where party contact is cross-tabulated with the Campaign Activity Index. One

TABLE IV. 1

The Relationship of Party Contact to Political Participation (%)[a]

Campaign Activity Index	Contact by One or Both Parties	No Party Contact	Total
Nonvoter	12	28	25
Spectator activities only	61	61	61
At least one gladiatorial activity	27	11	14
Total	100	100	100
Number of cases	(301)	(1,448)	(1,749)

[a]Data are from the 1956 study of the American electorate conducted by the Survey Research Center, University of Michigan.

can see in the table that among those contacted by a party there not only was a reduced percentage of nonvoters but an increased percentage of gladiators. When party contact was cross-tabulated with specific gladiatorial acts, the relationship was statistically significant only if the person was contacted by both political parties. This latter finding suggests that it may not be a single specific contact which stimulated gladiatorial action; rather, *persons who live in a milieu where party contact occurs regularly* (probably where there are strong parties and vigorous party competition) *are more likely to participate in politics.* Other studies show that *persons who are more interested in politics are more likely to know party workers* (Berelson, et al., 1954; McPhee & Glaser, 1962). *Party contact is most likely to increase turnout among long-time residents and among those least likely to vote* (Berelson, et al., 1954; McPhee & Glaser, 1962).

Contacting citizens individually is one of the most expensive (in terms of time) of all campaign activities. A get-out-the-vote experiment conducted by a graduate seminar at the University of Michigan required an investment of 400 hours to induce 39 persons out of 203 probable nonvoters to vote, a cost of 10 man-hours per vote (Eldersveld, 1956). Precinct captains for the dominant party in an area were found to be much more active in daily contacts with citizens than captains for minor parties. The higher the number of contacts, the more effective the captains were in increasing their party's vote for President (Rossi & Cutright, 1961).

Get-out-the-vote experiments showed that any kind of contact had some discernible impact on increasing turnout, but personal contact was the most effective (Eldersveld, 1956; Eldersveld & Dodge, 1954). It didn't seem to matter whether the personal contact was by student or party worker, by telephone or at the door. Those personally contacted retained the most information about the election and had the most interest in it. This suggests that the variable relationship may read this way: *personal contact stimulates interest and provides information which, in turn, increases the likelihood of coming out to vote.*

Contact by a friend carries the added attraction of a desire to please him as well as providing stimulation and information. In most cases, one would expect urging by a friend to be successful in getting a person to vote. Contact by a friend, however, may be even more important in getting a person to undertake gladiatorial activities. Research evidence on this point is very thin. In the Evanston survey of political participation, respondents were asked to agree or disagree with this statement: "A good friend would be able to encourage me to be active in politics." Gladiators were much more likely (71 per cent) to agree with the statement than spectators (42 per cent). A study of political elites in two communities showed that the urging of friends was a very important factor in getting persons involved in community decision-making, much more important than family influences (Jennings, 1964). Additional research may well confirm the trend of these data.

CHARACTERISTICS OF SPECIFIC ELECTIONS

Individuals differ in their perceptions of the same events; therefore, a very important factor for the political behavior of a person in an election is the way he perceives that election. He may see it as important or unimportant; he may think his vote counts or doesn't count; he may see it as a choice between Tweedledum and Tweedledee. It is important to note that individuals do not perceive in a vacuum: some elections are more important than others, some are more exciting than others, some are easier to understand than others. This has an aggregative effect, stimulating masses of people to perceive an election in a similar way.

Campbell (1960) has defined several differences between high-stimulus and low-stimulus elections. In a high-stimulus election, persons generally perceive that the vote will be close and, therefore, that their vote will count; they feel that the office being decided is an important one; they tend to perceive a clear choice between alternative candidates or parties; the candidates tend to be attractive; there is a high flow of campaign propaganda. A high-stimulus election brings out a relatively high turnout at the polls. Many of the voters are peripheral to the political process and tend to stay home in low-stimulus elections, for which only core voters tend to turn out. Each of the characteristics of a high-stimulus election is examined in turn.

Closeness of the Vote

This factor is highly relevant to the party-competition factor discussed above; competitive parties tend to produce close votes. The two factors are not identical, because close votes can occur in nonpartisan elections or in primary elections within a dominant party. We said above that party competition stimulates interest, and this, in turn, stimulates participation. Similarly, *a perception by people that the vote will be close piques their interest and strengthens their belief that their vote will count.* It is the individual's perception which is critical here; a widespread belief that the vote will be close is likely to bring out a high turnout, even if the vote should eventually be lopsided. Conversely, a widespread perception that one party or candidate will win depresses turnout, even if the vote turns out to be close. In the 1948 presidential election, when it was widely believed that Dewey would win, turnout dropped about 10 per cent from the normal percentage before and after that election (Milbrath, 1965, Fig. 2).

Perceptions of closeness of the vote may operate on two or more levels. Persons may perceive the local vote as very lopsided but the national vote as very close; the latter perception still tends to bring them to the polls, even though their local vote is not critical to the outcome. In Finland, turnout tended to be higher in those districts where more than 50 per cent of the vote was cast for a dominant party, but this tendency did not hold if citizens perceived that there was little chance to change the parties forming the national government (Allardt, 1956; Allardt & Bruun, 1956). In Britain in 1950, the highest turnouts tended to be found in closely contested constituencies or in those that were heavily dominated by Labor (Nicholas, 1951).

The potential relationship between closeness of the vote and turnout is weakened by two factors. Many people feel a duty to vote whether or not their vote is essential to the outcome of the election. Second, the activity of the local party organizations is very important in bringing out the vote, and the vigor of this activity is dependent on many factors in addition to the perceived closeness of the vote. In fact, a very strong and dominant party organization in an area can easily produce a whopping turnout without the added prodding of a close election. One naturally would expect party gladiators who know the vote will be close to bend every effort to help their side win, but sometimes they may work just as hard when they know they are sure winners.

These generalizations about the relationship between closeness of vote and turnout probably apply to gladiatorial activities as well. There is relatively little research on this. The Norwegian election study shows that *when the marginal value of a vote is high* (a few votes may turn the tide) *party organizations work harder to mobilize the vote* (Rokkan & Valen, 1962). Another scholar has speculated that close contests increase financial participation (Lane, 1959). As additional research relating closeness of vote to gladiatorial activities is conducted, our hypothesis can be confirmed or denied.

Importance of Elections
Persons are more likely to turn out for elections they perceive to be important (Campbell, 1960; Campbell, 1962). Individuals vary in their perceptions of the importance of a given election, but certain elections are widely perceived as

more important than others. **The more powerful the office being decided, the more important the election is likely to be perceived.** National elections are nearly always perceived as more important than local elections, and turnout is nearly always higher for national elections (Campbell, 1962; Converse & Dupeux, 1961; Lane, 1959; Milbrath, 1965; Robinson & Standing, 1960; Rokkan & Valen, 1962; Tingsten, 1937). The tendency for national elections to produce a higher turnout than local elections has been observed in five other Western nations in addition to the United States (Campbell, 1962; Converse & Dupeux, 1961; Lane, 1959; Milbrath, 1965; Robinson & Standing, 1960; Rokkan & Valen, 1962; Tingsten, 1937).

The trend for elections for higher office to produce higher turnout is so persistent that one scholar has suggested it might be wise to elect a chief executive (President, governor, mayor) at each election as one way to increase turnout for other offices (Lane, 1959). In Norway, the trend for national turnout to be greater than local was most pronounced in rural areas and in areas where the labor party was weakest (the Norwegian labor party is an effective agency for enlisting political participation from low SES persons) (Rokkan & Valen, 1962).

Crisis elections, which obviously are perceived as important, produce higher turnouts than noncrisis elections (Converse & Dupeux, 1961; Key, 1955; Lane, 1959; Lipset, 1960b). A study in France found that crises increased interest and psychological involvement in the election (Converse & Dupeux, 1961). In certain areas of Finland where the Communist party is strong (and therefore the election may be perceived as vital by non-Communist voters), the turnout by both Communist and non-Communist voters is high (Allardt & Bruun, 1956). *If a certain segment of the population perceives an election as important or vital, that segment will turn out at a rate higher than normal* (Lane, 1959). A good example of this in the United States is the abnormally high turnout of labor union members in the 1958 congressional elections in those states where so-called right to work laws (perceived as threats to union labor) were to be voted on. In addition to perceiving an election as important, *the citizen must also per-*

ceive the government as responding to his efforts if he is to be highly motivated to act (Campbell, 1962). The perception that an election is important seems most relevant to enlisting spectator activities such as voting (probably gladiators are more inclined to think every election is important), but the belief that the government responds to one's efforts may be more important for enlisting gladiatorial activity. (No data could be found relevant to these hypotheses.)

Clear Differences Between Alternatives

People are more likely to turn out for an election when clear differences are perceived between alternatives than when the alternatives are unclear (Campbell, 1960; Campbell, 1962; Rokkan & Valen, 1962). Clarity of alternatives seems especially important in mobilizing citizens who usually stand on the periphery of politics and do not participate (Campbell, 1960; Rokkan & Valen, 1962). When the alternatives are clear, the costs of collecting information and making a decision are reduced. This was suggested as one possible explanation of why turnout is usually higher for general elections than for primary elections (Matthews & Prothro, 1963b). A study of Negroes in Florida politics reported that when the issues are blurred, or lack relevance to the problems of Negroes, the interest of the individual Negro drops, and the cohesion of Negroes as a voting bloc is reduced (Price, 1955). A study of a Swedish election showed that the stands on issues of party followers became much more polarized as the campaign progressed (Särlvik, 1961a).

If all the alternatives in an election are perceived as unattractive, turnout is likely to be lowered even further than normal (Campbell, 1962). Many people perceived both United States presidential candidates (Truman and Dewey) as unattractive in 1948, whereas both candidates (Eisenhower and Stevenson) were perceived as attractive by many persons in 1952; turnout was unusually low in 1948 and unusually high in 1952 (Campbell, et al., 1954; Campbell, et al., 1960; Davies, 1954). The reader should keep in mind that clarity and attractiveness of alternatives apply to issues and parties as well as to candidates; all three factors interact to produce the total image of an election. The presence of candidates does seem to lend a spark to an election. A study of election returns from several countries showed that **turnout generally was lower for referenda and other noncandidate elections than for elections with candidates** (Tingsten, 1937). Clarity and attractiveness of alternatives mainly affect election-day turnout and other spectator activities. Gladiators, by virtue of being more involved in the political contest, generally perceive much clearer differences between sides than do spectators. Not only is their knowledge greater and perhaps more accurate, but also they have a need to justify their stand both to themselves and to persons whom they may try to convince that they are right. It was found in a study of national convention delegates that there are much wider differences in policy views between Democratic and Republican party leaders than between Democratic and Republican party followers (ordinary citizens) (McClosky, et al., 1960).

Flow of Propaganda

Some campaigns are characterized by a heavier exchange of propaganda between the contesting teams than other campaigns. Some scattered bits of evidence suggest that *the heavier the flow of propaganda, the higher the voting turnout* (Eldersveld, 1956; Eldersveld & Dodge, 1954; Pesonen, 1961). The evidence is not extensive enough to know whether this is a simple linear relationship or whether it is curvilinear. Certainly, if one starts from the bottom (no campaign propaganda at all), succeeding increments of propaganda will produce some increase in turnout. But is there a saturation point beyond which additional propaganda has little or no effect? It may even be possible that propaganda flow could become so heavy as to offend citizens, thus driving them away from the polls instead of attracting them. Much more adequate evidence is needed before we can specify the nature of the relationship between level of propaganda and turnout.

REGIONAL DIFFERENCES WITHIN A POLITICAL SYSTEM

Little research attention has been given to region itself as a variable in political behavior research. Often regional differences coincide with differences in social and economic factors or with differences in political system, and these are treated as variables rather than region. Without evidence directly relevant to the point, it is difficult to say whether or not region by itself is a differentiating variable. The following should be taken only as suggestive.

Studies of the national electorate in the United States have repeatedly found that the South as a region acts differently from the rest of the country (Campbell, et al., 1954; Campbell, et al., 1960). These studies consistently show that *persons from the South are significantly less likely to vote and slightly less likely to participate in gladiatorial activities than persons living in other regions of the country.* The endeavor in the South to keep Negroes from voting by no means accounts for all of the difference. The party system is less competitive in the South. More persons are engaged in agriculture. Industrialization is less advanced there, and income and educational levels are lower. In addition, it is conceivable that differences in climate, in topography, and in political history and traditions also contribute to this regional difference. It is impossible with the data available to sort out and weigh the relative contribution of these several factors. The Norwegian election studies show a lower level of political participation in the northern region, which seems to be due to severe problems in transportation and communication occasioned by difficult topography and inclement weather (Rokkan & Valen, 1962).

NONELECTORAL AND NONPARTY FACTORS IN POLITICAL SETTING

Not all political activity is oriented toward elections and party competition. Much interelection activity is designed to communicate policy preferences to official decision-makers. The amount of this activity depends partly on the pain felt from the social ills persons want corrected and partly on the perceptions citizens have of the responsiveness of officials to their pleas. *Persons who perceive themselves or their group as having an impact on public policy are more likely to communicate their policy preferences to officials than are those perceiving little or no impact* (Lane, 1959). Certain political leaders tend to invite messages from citizens and generally receive an increased flow of communications as a result (Sussman, 1959). Members of Congress who do so are known as those who "court mail." A study in Finland shows that political leaders who take an interest in the people and their problems stimulate a higher level of communicative activity from citizens to officials (Allardt & Pesonen, 1960). Persons in certain environments may perceive that their messages are not being listened to and may choose extraordinary means, such as protest demonstrations, to help make sure that the messages are received.

In addition to using routine and extraordinary means to communicate their policy desires to public officials, citizens of most countries have set up institutions to aggregate their collective interests and to communicate their policy desires. These institutions are variously known as special-interest groups, pressure groups, or lobby groups. They provide a quality and intensity of policy representation that cannot be achieved by political parties or individuals acting separately. In the United States, these groups often take the extra step of hiring a special envoy, called a lobbyist, to spend full time at the seat of government acting as a communication link between his group and the government (Milbrath, 1963). Having organizations of this type available in the political environment provides an additional channel for participation in politics. More than a third of United States citizens belong to one or more of these intermediary political groups, but probably less than half of them are active in their group (only 4 or 5 per cent of Americans are members of political parties). Many of the same factors that draw persons into electoral activity also draw persons into group activity.[2] It is difficult, however, to go beyond this kind of broad generalization about a propensity for being active in groups. Although there have been many studies of interest groups and interest-group activity,[3] there is very little research on the specific

[2] See footnote 5, Chapter I, for citations to studies showing general group activity correlated with political activity.

[3] See the bibliography to Milbrath (1963).

factors recruiting persons for membership and participation in interest groups.

This chapter has dealt only with the relationship between the political sector of the environment and participation in politics. In explaining this relationship, it has often been necessary to show the linkage of the political environment to participation via intermediary personal factors like attitudes, beliefs, and personality traits. This same kind of intermediary linkage is often necessary in the following chapter when we deal with the relationship between social-position factors and political participation.

V

POLITICAL PARTICIPATION AS A
FUNCTION OF SOCIAL POSITION

THE GREATEST QUANTITY of research on political participation has related that behavior to social-position variables. In part, this is because social-position and other demographic variables are so visible and so readily measured. They are included in nearly every study as a matter of custom and convenience. A related reason is that social-position variables "stand for" many of the attitudinal and personality variables, discussed earlier, which are so difficult to measure. Social-position variables, such as class or place of residence, do not "cause" any specific behavior in the sense that they are requisites for, or the immediate antecedents of, given acts. Social conditions, however, do form personalities, beliefs, and attitudes which, in turn, do "cause" (are requisite to) specific acts such as participation in politics.

It is a simple matter, then, to find correlational relationships between social-position variables and political participation, but the reader should keep in mind that the effects of social-position variables must be mediated through personality, beliefs, and opinions. Social environment also can affect the behavior through the stimuli which it presents to behaving organisms (this was discussed in Chapter II). The reader should keep both channels of influence in mind throughout the following discussion.

SOCIAL POSITION TOWARD THE CENTER OR
PERIPHERY OF SOCIETY

A general way to discuss the relationship of social position to political participation is to plot social position along a central-peripheral dimension. This is superior for heuristic purposes to the more commonly used social class or socioeconomic status. For one thing, the center-periphery concept incorporates other variables in addition to SES, such as length of time at a given residence, amount of group activity, urban-rural residence, and integration into the community. Another reason is that position on the center-periphery dimension is more than an objective fact, it is also a psychological feeling of being close to the center of things or of being out on the periphery. This feeling of closeness to or distance from the center is an important correlate of political participation. Feeling or perception is closely entwined with reality here; the person whose life circumstances have placed him close to the center (as determined by an impartial observer) is quite likely to *feel* closer to the center than is a person whose life circumstances have placed him on the periphery (as determined by an impartial observer).

There is no objective center which every observer would immediately recognize as such, and this means it is necessary to try to define the concept. Defining it one way might show a stronger relationship to political participation than defining it another. We shall look at several definitions advanced by scholars which differ in specifics but which have many similarities. The precise nature of the concept may still be a bit vague at the conclusion of that examination, but the broad outlines of the dimension will be visible, and that will be adequate for our purposes.

Lane has defined centrality largely in terms of communication (1959, p. 196). Centrally located persons are more accessible, more likely to be informed, partake in more discussions, belong to more organizations, are more likely to be opinion leaders.[1] A study of decision-making in a housing project showed that apartment dwellers located at a cross-path or at the bottom of the stairs were more likely to become involved in a controversy over self-government for the project (Festinger, et al., 1950). Another aspect of Lane's definition of centrality is that the centrally located person is liked by many others, especially other "central" persons.

[1] This is similar to Berelson, et al. (1954).

As a consequence, he is involved in many more interactions and receives many more communications.

Rokkan and Valen (1962) have defined communes in Norway, instead of people, as central or peripheral. Peripheral communes have many persons engaged in primary occupations such as fishing and agriculture, whereas central communes have more secondary (manufacturing) and especially more tertiary (service) occupations. Peripheral communes lost, and central communes gained population. Per capita income is lower in peripheral communes than in central communes. Peripheral communes have more small farms and less favorable tax rates because of many subsistence incomes. Peripheral communes are relatively isolated from existing transport networks. This is a reasonably good operational definition of centrality-peripherality in Norway, but one would expect other factors, as well, to be relevant in other societies.

Sociologists sometimes speak of the "underdog" in society (Knupfer, 1947); this is the socially and economically underprivileged. The operational definition of the underdog is essentially socioeconomic status: underdogs have low income, little education, low prestige, and feel that they have little power. They are similar to the persons discussed as alienated in Chapter III. The underdog might be thought of as on the periphery of society, while the top dog is at the center.

Agger and Ostrom isolated a community role they termed "active advisor" (Agger, 1956b; Agger & Ostrom, 1956). Such persons are in close contact with the "top leadership" in the community. The characteristics of these active advisors are very similar to those generally defined here as persons near the center of society: they have higher educational attainment, membership in more groups, greater length of residence in the community, plan to continue to live in the community, read more out-of-town newspapers, associate more with school or governmental officials, are more likely to have held public office, are more likely to be men than women, and are not likely to be young persons.

Lazarsfeld and Katz developed the concept of "opinion

leader" (Berelson, et al., 1954; Katz, 1957-1958; Katz & Lazarsfeld, 1955; Lazarsfeld, et al., 1944). Opinion leaders are important communication links in the message flows of a society. They attend more to the mass media and communicate more with leaders; in turn, when requested, they pass this information on to others who are not so closely tied in to the communications system. They have many of the characteristics of persons near the center: higher SES, strategic social location (to receive and send messages), high integration into social groupings, high competence (highly correlated with education), high gregariousness, more activity in groups, greater interest in a subject (public affairs), greater exposure to media, and they personify certain values (are admired). The intimate relationship between position factors and personality factors is illustrated by this listing of characteristics of opinion leaders.

The general central-peripheral dimension should now be visible to the reader. Persons close to the center occupy an environmental position which naturally links them into the communications network involved in policy decisions for the society. They become identified with the body politic. They receive from and send more communications to other persons near the center. They have a higher rate of social interaction, and they are active in more groups than persons on the periphery. This central position increases the likelihood that they will develop personality traits, beliefs, and attitudes which facilitate participation in politics. There are many more political stimuli in their environment, and this increases the number of opportunities for them to participate. (See Figure 4, Chapter I for a conceptual scheme of these relationships.)

One of the most thoroughly substantiated propositions in all of social science is that **persons near the center of society are more likely to participate in politics than persons near the periphery** (Agger, 1956b; Agger & Goldrich, 1958; Agger & Ostrom, 1956; Berelson, et al., 1954; Buchanan, 1956; Campbell, et al., 1954; Campbell, et al., 1960; Campbell & Kahn, 1952; Dogan, 1961; Glaser, 1959; Gronseth, 1955; Guttsman, 1951; Karlsson, 1958a; Katz & Lazarsfeld, 1955;

Kitt & Gleicher, 1950; Kornhauser, et al., 1956; Lane, 1959; Lazarsfeld, et al., 1944; Lipset, 1950; Lipset, 1960b; Lipset, et al., 1954; Marvick & Nixon, 1961; Masumi, 1961; M. Miller, 1952; Pesonen, 1960; Pesonen, 1961; Riesman & Glazer, 1950; Rokkan & Valen, 1962). *Persons near the center encounter more stimuli enticing them to participate, and they receive more social support from their peers when they do participate.* Children growing up in homes located near the center are more likely to develop personalities, beliefs, and attitudes facilitating their entry into politics (Dogan, 1961; Guttsman, 1951; Marvick & Nixon, 1961). Furthermore, *persons at the center tend to recruit new political gladiators from their acquaintances at the center* (Guttsman, 1951; Kuroda, 1964). Decision-makers at the center are more likely to respond to communications coming from other persons near the center (Lane, 1959). *Persons near the periphery are less likely to send communications to the center* (Lane, 1959).

A corollary of all this is the finding that *stability in location and occupation across generations tends to increase political participation* (Lipset, 1950; Lipset, 1960b; Pesonen, 1961). This generalization probably is more true of persons in high-status positions than of low-status persons. A person in a menial position is unlikely to participate no matter how many generations were in the same position. The proposition is also more likely to hold for traditional societies than for highly mobile industrialized societies like the United States. Whether a person had the same occupation status as his father or had risen or fallen in status showed no consistent relationship to the Campaign Activity Index on the Survey Research Center's 1956 Election data.

SOCIOECONOMIC STATUS (SES) OR CLASS

It will not be necessary, for our purposes, to distinguish status and class; they will be treated as roughly the same concept. Status or class differences imply not only that some persons have more of the goods of life than others, but also that some persons are looked up to more than others. Status differences are found in every society, even though the components of status and the ways of measuring it differ from society to society. What is valued and looked up to in one society may not be valued in another.

Yet, no matter what things are valued in status and no matter how status is measured, it seems clear that persons of high status are close to the center of society and persons of low status usually are on the periphery. Center-periphery, as defined above, is a broader concept than status, so the two are not identical, but the correlation between them is very high.

In Western industrialized societies in the mid-twentieth century, SES is generally conceived of as having three components: education, income, and occupation. These three components are themselves highly intercorrelated, but they are sufficiently different to warrant measuring them separately and including all three in a combined "objective" index of class or status. In a typical index of this type (different scholars use somewhat different weightings), persons who scored high on all three factors would be placed in the upper SES. Those who scored high on two factors but medium or low on one factor would be in the next rank. Those who scored high on only one factor would be in the next rank, and so forth. The index is called "objective" because the researcher places the respondent in a particular status after he has gathered the relevant data on the person.

In contrast, a "subjective" measure of class allows the respondent to select the class that he thinks he falls into. One of the first questions of this type might have read something like this: "Do you usually think of yourself as being part of the upper class, the upper-middle class, the lower-middle class, or the lower class?" Researchers soon discovered several difficulties with this type of question: (1) some people never thought about class; (2) few people had the pride to place themselves in the upper class; (3) almost no one had the lack of pride to call himself lower class. Modern survey researchers now use a series of questions reading something like this: "There is a lot of discussion about class these days. Do you ever think of yourself as belonging to a class?" "If you had to pick a class for yourself, would you say you are middle class or working class?" "Do you think you are in the upper part of the _____ class or just average _____ class?" A small percentage of respondents in the United States refuse to pick any class, sometimes insisting there are no classes in a democracy. Most respondents, however, give answers that are readily codable into one of the four categories produced by the questions: upper middle, lower middle, upper working, and lower working.[2]

Naturally, some respondents "misperceive" their class when their judgment is compared to the scholar's "objective" measurement, but most correlations between the two types of measures are rather high. Most people do accurately perceive their class status. More importantly, subjective perception of class may be as significant, or more significant, an indication of behavioral predisposition than the person's "objective" status. People tend to take on the norms and behavior patterns of the class they aspire to join. As one might imagine, many people aspire upward and take on middle-class values; almost no one aspires downward. No matter how class is measured, studies consistently show that **higher-class persons are more likely to participate in politics than lower-class persons** (Agger, et al., 1964; Allardt & Pesonen, 1960; Campbell, et al., 1954; Campbell, et al., 1960; Connelly & Field, 1944; Dahl, 1961; Erbe, 1964; Eulau, 1962; Foskett, 1955; McPhee & Glaser, 1962; Tingsten, 1937; Woodward & Roper, 1950. In addition, many of the citations on pp. 113-14 are relevant here). This proposition has been confirmed in at least six countries. A recent inventory of behavioral science propositions attributes this finding to three factors: (1) higher-class persons are better educated; (2) they are more likely to perceive that they have a stake in politics; (3) they are more likely to interact with persons active in politics (Berelson & Steiner, 1964).

The relationship between self class identification and the Campaign Activity Index (on an American sample) is shown in Table V.I. With rise in class, the percentage of nonvoters not only declines, but the percentage of gladiators rises equal-

[2] For an interesting political analysis working with these categories, see Eulau (1962).

TABLE V. 1

Campaign Activity Index by Self Class Identification [a]

| | Self Class Identification (%) | | | | |
Campaign Activity Index	Average Working Class	Upper Working Class	Average Middle Class	Upper Middle Class	Total
Nonvoters	34	16	15	12	25
Spectator activities only	58	68	65	57	61
At least one gladiatorial activity	8	16	20	31	14
Total	100	100	100	100	100
Number of cases	(887)	(146)	(508)	(118)	(1,659)
tau beta correlation = .25					

[a]Data are from the 1956 study of the American electorate conducted by the Survey Research Center, University of Michigan.

ly. The correlation of .25 between the two variables is of approximately the same magnitude as the correlation between education and the CAI, and is a bit higher than the correlations between income and the CAI (.20) and between occupation status and the CAI (.20). These data suggest that subjective class feelings are as good an indication of behavioral predisposition toward politics as an "objective" measure of class. In the Evanston survey mentioned previously, self class identification was significantly related to the difference between apathetics and spectators but was not significantly related to the difference between spectators and gladiators (Jensen, 1960). Being a subjective measure of class, it may operate somewhat differently in a single community that is relatively homogeneous in status than in a national sample.

Upwardly mobile persons, those attempting to improve their class status, *may become active in politics as part of their effort to move upward* (Dogan, 1961; Marvick & Nixon, 1961). This generalization mainly applies to gladiatorial rather than to spectator activities. Gladiatorial activity may bring the prize of public office and the opportunity to be close to top decision-makers. Spectator activity alone would not be likely to produce such status-improving effects. On the other hand, some scholars have speculated that persons already at the top of the status ladder may disdain gladiatorial activity in politics (Mitchell, 1959). Although this may accurately characterize many high SES persons, one can think of enough high-status persons who are also political gladiators to suspect that the percentage of high-status persons who are gladiators is no less than the percentage of middle-status persons.

A study in Finland reports that after the economic level of the underprivileged northern counties was raised, the level of political participation also went up (Pesonen, 1961). It seems that persons need to rise above a mere subsistence level before politics can become a factor in their lives (Davies, 1963). This generalization cannot be extended very far, however; not every rise in standard of living produces a corresponding rise in political participation. Data from the 1956 election study of the Survey Research Center show that persons with an occupational status that is higher than their father's, or that is higher than it was earlier in their own life, tend to rank no higher on the CAI than persons who did not rise in status. These data also show, however, that *persons with an occupational status that is drastically lower than their father's are less likely to participate in politics.* This relationship may reflect a difference in competence: a son who takes an occupation several rungs lower in status than his father's very likely is less competent than his father (we saw in Chapter III that competent persons are more likely to participate in politics). Available data are not adequate to check this interpretation.

Some persons have an indeterminate status; perhaps their education is high but their income is low, or vice versa. Perhaps they continue to live in a poor neighborhood when their educational and income achievements would enable them to move to a better one. Some scholars speak of such persons as having "cross-pressures" in their status and report that they are less likely to vote than persons who are not cross-pressured (Lazarsfeld, et al., 1944; Lenski, 1956; Lipset, 1960b). Presumably, the cross-pressure arises from the tendency for one aspect of their status to incline them in a

Republican direction, while the other aspect of their status inclines them toward the Democrats. They resolve the dilemma by not voting at all. No data were found relating cross-pressures in status to gladiatorial activity.

Studies in countries with status-polarized party systems (multiple parties that split along class lines) show that *political participation, especially voting turnout, is higher in communes which are homogeneous in politics, socioeconomic status, and economic activity* (e.g., all fishing or all manufacturing) (Allardt & Bruun, 1956; Allardt & Pesonen, 1960; Lipset, 1950; Pesonen, 1960; Pesonen, 1961; Rokkan, 1962b; Rokkan & Campbell, 1960). In Finland, where both Swedish and Finnish are official languages, communes that are homogeneous in language have higher turnout (Allardt & Bruun, 1956). *In societies with residential segregation by SES* (SES homogeneity within political units), *the normal tendency for high SES persons to be more likely to participate is reduced* (Allardt & Bruun, 1956; Lipset, 1960b; Rokkan, 1962b; Tingsten, 1937). One can guess that without status differences to inhibit their feeling of competence and importance, lower-class persons are more likely to become willing political workers. If this homogeneous group should also have its own political party (as we saw earlier is true of some areas in Norway), that party would recruit and train workers from within its own stratum (Rokkan, 1962b).

Changes in the socioeconomic structure of an area affect political behavior by slowly affecting the attitudes of the persons who live there. There usually is a time lag. Areas in Indiana that changed from agricultural to industrial continued their old voting patterns for several elections, showing only gradual erosion of the old patterns (Key & Munger, 1959). The southern states are shifting rapidly from an agricultural to an industrial economy, but a rise in the percentage turnout at elections lags about a decade behind (Milbrath, 1965). West Virginia, which has been industrialized for some time, but which is now having considerable problems with poverty and unemployment, continues to have one of the highest turnout percentages in the United States (Milbrath, 1965). Economic modernization is a potent, if slow, force affecting political patterns. Studies in Norway and Japan show that *as patterns of employment shifted from largely primary economic activities* (fishing, agriculture, forestry) *to secondary* (manufacturing) *and tertiary* (services), *more and more persons who had formerly stayed outside the political process were mobilized into the electorate* (Masumi, 1961; Rokkan, 1962a; Rokkan & Valen, 1962). As these areas became more industrialized, more of the political contesting was carried out through political parties: party membership rose, parties took the job of candidate recruitment, and nonpartisan elections tended to fall into disuse (Masumi, 1961; Rokkan & Valen, 1962). As industrialization progressed in France, more and more persons with middle-class origins were elected to the French Assembly (Dogan, 1961).

We have little information about what happens to political participation during times of depression. During the great depression of the thirties, the number of persons offering themselves as candidates for public office in Indiana rose; later, during World War II, the number of candidates dropped off (Standing & Robinson, 1958). The researchers suggested that during periods of high unemployment the lure of public office (with its certain salary) substantially improves. Another scholar, after checking voting turnout figures over a considerable period of time, could find no relationship between depressions and voting turnout (Lane, 1959).

Income

Similar to the finding for SES, studies in many Western countries show that **income is positively correlated with political participation** (Agger & Ostrom, 1956; Campbell, et al., 1954; Campbell, et al., 1960; Campbell & Kahn, 1952; Connelly & Field, 1944; Dahl, 1961; Gronseth, 1955; Korchin, 1946; Lane, 1959; Lipset, 1960b; M. Miller, 1952; Riesman & Glazer, 1950; Tingsten, 1937; Valen, 1961). The tau beta correlation between income and the Campaign Activity Index on the 1956 election data is .22. The Evanston survey showed that middle-income persons are significantly more likely to be active in politics than low-income persons, but that high-income persons are not significantly more likely to be active

than middle-income persons (Jensen, 1960).[3] Lane, in study-
ing some turnout figures by income levels, suggested "a kind
of declining marginal productivity of income on voting" (1959,
p. 326). For each thousand-dollar increment in income, the
absolute increase and the rate of increase in turnout declined.
It is partly because of this factor that income correlates somewhat less highly with political participation than some other
indices of SES.

Income has another interesting characteristic: it relates
significantly with some specific political acts but not with
others. On the 1956 election data there was a slight, but not
statistically significant, trend for higher-income persons to be
more likely to work for a party, join a political club, attend
meetings, and proselyte. The percentage of participants was
clearly higher only in the two highest income brackets ($7,500
and above). On the other hand, there was a consistent trend,
which was statistically significant, for higher-income persons
to be more likely to wear a button or put a sticker on the
car and to give money to a party or candidate. Fully 30 per
cent of those in the highest income bracket ($10,000 and
over) contributed money, compared to 10 per cent for the
entire sample. It is easy to understand why rich people would
be more likely to give money than poor people; it is not so
clear why they should be more likely to wear a button or
display a sticker. The data do not suggest a likely interpretation, but one can speculate that publicly identifying one's
partisan or candidate preference requires high self-esteem,
and high-income persons are more likely to have high self-
esteem. It was suggested by another scholar that higher-
income persons not only are more likely to give money, but
they also are more likely to initiate direct contacts with public officials (Lane, 1959), which again suggests high self-
esteem. A ranking of states on per capita personal income
shows a positive correlation with a ranking of the states on
percentage of voting turnout (Milbrath, 1965).[4]

[3] Kuroda (1964) found in a Japanese community that income did not relate significantly to participation.

[4] Lane (1959) reported no relationship when attempting a similar correlation.

Education

A trend for those with higher education to be more likely to participate in politics has also been found in many Western countries (Agger & Goldrich, 1958; Agger & Ostrom, 1956; Agger, et al., 1964; Allardt & Pesonen, 1960; Almond & Verba, 1963; Benny, et al., 1956; Berelson, et al., 1954; Buchanan, 1956; Campbell, 1962; Campbell, et al., 1954; Converse & Dupeux, 1961; Dahl, 1961; Gronseth, 1955; Jensen, 1960; Key, 1961; Kornhauser, et al., 1956; Kuroda, 1964; Lane, 1959; Lipset, 1960b; McPhee & Glaser, 1962; M. Miller, 1952; Sussman, 1959; Woodward & Roper, 1950). The Survey Research Center's 1956 election data and the Evanston survey both show a tau beta correlation of .25 between education and an index of participation. The five-nation study shows that educational differences were more important in accounting for differences in participation in Italy, Germany, and Mexico than in the United Kingdom and the United States (Almond & Verba, 1963, p. 121). The investigators concluded from patterns found in all five nations that education has a greater impact on political behavior than the other components of socioeconomic status (income and occupation) (p. 400).[5]

Why does education have such a strong affect on political behavior? The five-nation study has done the most thorough research on that question. The findings are very clear, they hold in all five nations, and they parallel many points already made in this book. The summary is so clear and inclusive that it deserves quotation at length. The chapter citations are to chapters in *The Civic Culture*.

(1) the more educated person is more aware of the impact of government on the individual than is the person of less education (chapter 3);

(2) The more educated individual is more likely to report that he follows politics and pays attention to election campaigns than is the individual of less education (chapter 3);

(3) The more educated individual has more political information (chapter 3);

[5] Agger & Ostrom (1956) also reported education to be more significant than income.

(4) The more educated individual has opinions on a wider range of political subjects; the focus of his attention to politics is wider (chapter 3);

(5) The more educated individual is more likely to engage in political discussion (chapter 4);

(6) The more educated individual feels free to discuss politics with a wider range of people (chapter 4). Those with less education are more likely to report that there are many people with whom they avoid such discussions;

(7) The more educated individual is more likely to consider himself capable of influencing the government; this is reflected both in responses to questions on what one could do about an unjust law (chapter 7) and in respondent's scores on the subjective competence scale (chapter 9).

The above list refers to specifically political orientations, which vary the same way in all five nations. In addition, our evidence shows that:

(8) The more educated individual is more likely to be a member—and an active member—of some organization (chapter 11); and

(9) The more educated individual is more likely to express confidence in his social environment: to believe that other people are trustworthy and helpful (chapter 10) (Almond & Verba, 1963, pp. 380-381).

In Norway, which has status-polarized parties, the familiar relationship between education and participation holds for voting but not for gladiatorial activities. Since each party must recruit workers from within its own socioeconomic status, persons from all strata are equally likely to be recruited for gladiatorial activities. This finding leads to the speculation that where partisan contesting is not very vigorous, the relationship of participation to education will be more marked than where parties contest vigorously (Rokkan & Campbell, 1960).

Education showed a consistent and significant positive relationship with each of the specific political acts included in the 1956 election study (and in the CAI). Education seems to be especially important as a prerequisite for demanding political jobs; several studies show that persons holding important public office are very likely to be well educated (college and professional degrees) (Anderson, 1935; Buck, 1963; Dogan, 1961; Schlesinger, 1957; Valen, 1961).

Occupation

Occupation is a somewhat more tricky variable to interpret than education or income. What kinds of occupational distinctions are meaningful, and how can one compute quantitative differences in occupation (as one can for income and education)? A traditional distinction, which is rather broad and vague, is between white-collar and blue-collar occupations, but the color of his collar is not a sure guide to the most relevant characteristics of a person's occupation. This distinction produces inconclusive results when it is related to political participation. Some studies (Allardt & Bruun, 1956) show white-collar persons to be more likely to participate than blue-collar, while other studies (Jensen, 1960) show no relationship.

Another way of handling occupation is to rank the statuses of the various occupations. Occupations closer to the center usually are perceived as having higher status than those on the periphery. One way to create a status ranking is to have a random sample of citizens rate the prestige of various occupations. Such ratings have quite high inter-rater reliability, suggesting that there are widely shared beliefs about the prestige of occupations. A categorization based on such ratings was used to make an occupation status index for respondents in the 1956 election study. This index showed a clear tendency for higher-status persons to be more likely to be active in politics; the tau beta correlation with the CAI was .20. Several other studies report that **persons of higher occupational status are more likely to participate in politics** (Agger & Ostrom, 1956; Berelson, et al., 1954; Bonham, 1952; Buck, 1963; Campbell & Kahn, 1952; Connelly & Field, 1944; Dahl, 1961; Gronseth, 1955; Korchin, 1946; Lane, 1959; McPhee & Glaser, 1962). The exception for Norway, discussed under education, also applies here. The status-polarized party system there requires recruiting for political workers within occupations at all statuses; therefore, the over-all relationship between occupation status and participation is not very pronounced in Norway (Rokkan & Campbell, 1960).

One can also ask the question: "What is it about occupation that might facilitate or hinder political participation?" This is likely to produce a different type of categorization than that discussed above. Lane has suggested that these characteristics of jobs facilitate political participation: (1) the development and use of social and intellectual skills that might carry over to politics; (2) opportunity to interact with like-minded others; (3) higher than average stakes in governmental policy; (4) roles on the job that carry over to public service (1959, p. 334). A study of local party officials shows that a higher than normal percentage of them had come from occupations with "brokerage roles" (occupations requiring the person to relate smoothly with other people) (Boynton & Bowman, 1964).

The following four criteria, that theoretically seemed important in determining whether a person in an occupation would become active in politics, were used to create an index of occupational propensity toward politics.[6] (1) Does the job provide an opportunity (freedom of schedule and blocks of time) for political action? (2) Does the job require or develop skills (largely verbal) that can be transferred to politics? (3) Is the job sufficiently affected by political decisions that job occupants would feel it important to become active in politics to protect or enhance their position? (4) Does the position become vulnerable if the occupant engages in politics; in other words, might a job-holder have to pay a cost in anxiety or defense if he should participate? Specific jobs were rated as high, medium, or low on each of the criteria by a board of judges. Simple weights were applied (1, 2, 3, with scoring for the last criterion reversed), and scores were summed for the four criteria. Lawyers, as an example, were scored high on the first three criteria, but medium on the last.

Inter-rater reliability was satisfactory, and the resulting index did correlate significantly with the CAI. However, the over-all correlation was no higher than that between occupation status and the CAI.[7] As might be expected from the

---

[6]Robert Boynton collaborated with the author on this.

[7]Neuman (1964) found that time differences in availability of leisure in different occupations had a weak impact on political participation.

criteria employed, the index showed a stronger relationship with gladiatorial activities than with spectator activities. At the highest ranks of the index, 38 per cent of the persons had engaged in at least one gladiatorial activity compared with 14 per cent for the entire sample. This pattern, for those on the top rank of the index to be much more likely to participate, held for each of the specific acts included in the CAI. This difference in top-rank behavior suggests, although we would need more and better data to be confident, that a high rank on all or nearly all of the criteria are needed before a person feels that the door is wide open to gladiatorial activity.

Turning now to somewhat more specific occupations, several studies show that **professional persons are the most likely to get involved in politics** (Anderson, 1935; Buck, 1963; Guttsman, 1951; Jensen, 1960; M. Miller, 1952; Schlesinger, 1957). This generalization seems especially true of political officeholding, being very evident for higher offices. It very probably would not hold for a setting where political activity, or the kind of office held, is not well respected. The Evanston survey showed professionals most likely to be active in politics, followed by businessmen, clerical, skilled, and unskilled workers in that order (Jensen, 1960). In Anglo-Saxon countries and in France, lawyers are especially likely to seek office and be active in other ways in politics; this pattern is not so prevalent in other countries, however. Almost half of the state governors in the United States from 1870 to 1950 (456 of 995) were practicing lawyers (Schlesinger, 1957). Occupations of members of the British Parliament have followed a trend away from landowning and toward professional occupations (Buck, 1963; Guttsman, 1951). There is a pattern in some countries for government employees to be very active politically (Lipset, 1960b; Tingsten, 1937). Whether or not this occurs may depend on possible legal prohibitions against political activity by public employees. The Hatch Act (1940) controls the political activities of employees of the federal government in the United States. Certainly, the public nature of their job means that government job-holders have an important stake in political outcomes.

Businessmen, compared to the rest of the population,

tend to be quite active in politics, although there is variation from business to business and perhaps also from community to community. A study of the political activity of Philadelphia businessmen reported these findings: A high proportion vote and contribute money, as a matter of course (40 per cent contributed money as compared to 10 per cent for a national sample) (Janosik, 1962). The percentage of businessmen who worked in a campaign (8 per cent) was just a little higher than the national average (3 or 4 per cent) and is a normal percentage for upper-middle SES persons. There were no public office-holders among these businessmen. They tended to have a positive attitude toward politics and politicians, tended to be optimistic about politics, and tended slightly to inhibit political discussion for fear of offending associates. Top business executives were more likely to be active in politics than middle- and lower-level executives. Another study of the effects of political training classes, designed to involve businessmen in politics, reported modest to poor results for the training (Hacker & Aberbach, 1962). The positive attractions to politics often did not compensate for the costs of political action (especially diversion of time and energy).

Most studies show laboring persons disinclined, on the whole, to become involved actively in politics. There are exceptions to this generalization in countries with strong working-class movements and parties. We saw above how effective the Norwegian labor party is in enlisting political activity from laboring men. In the United States, labor unions have some success in mobilizing their members for political action, but the result is not very impressive; this effort will be discussed later under group memberships. Certain aspects of a laboring man's job make it difficult for him to become active in politics, especially to undertake gladiatorial activity. He has a fixed work schedule, making it difficult to be free for meetings. His job usually does not emphasize or teach verbal skills that can be transferred to political action. The relevance of political outcomes for his income and job satisfaction is often not very clear. Farmers tend to have the lowest levels of political participation of all occupational groupings (Campbell, et al., 1960). The major reason for this is grounded in the relative isolation of rural life.

URBAN-RURAL

In the definitional terms for center-periphery discussed at the beginning of this chapter, it is clear that the urban dweller is generally closer to the center of most societies than is the rural dweller. This is largely due to the enhanced opportunity for interaction and communication that the urban dweller has when compared to rural people. Campbell was quoted on urban opportunities for communication in Chapter II (p. 42); a few additional remarks are germane:

> We . . . find very low levels of political interest and involvement among farmers in the United States. Despite the widespread ownership of automobiles and television sets by rural people, farm life in America is not only physically but socially remote. The typical farmer not only lives apart from his neighbors but has relatively little formal association with them. Most American farmers belong to no farm organizations and few of those who do express any great interest in them (Campbell, 1962, pp. 13-14).

It has been found in many studies in many societies that **farmers are less likely to become active in politics than city dwellers** (Berelson, et al., 1954; Campbell, 1962; Campbell, et al., 1960; McPhee & Glaser, 1962; Pesonen, 1960; Rokkan & Campbell, 1960; Rokkan & Valen, 1962; Tingsten, 1937, in all four Scandinavian countries). In addition to the communication disadvantages of the rural setting, another reason for the urban-rural difference is the striking difference in political activity levels of rural and urban women (Rokkan & Campbell, 1960). Women from families engaged in primary economic activity (agriculture, forestry, fishing) are much less likely· to participate in politics. Women in a primary economy stay close to home and often are involved in production. This not only leaves little time for politics, but also limits social interaction to family members (once again, social interaction seems to be a central variable). An additional factor is that primary economies tend to be more tradition-oriented, and it is a strong tradition to think of politics as "man's work." As a greater proportion of the economic activity in a locality becomes secondary and tertiary, the differences in participation between men and women are reduced. Women in urban areas in Norway are just as likely to vote as men, they are just as likely as men to take part in party affairs, and they are more likely to become candidates for office than rural women, even though urban men are still more likely to become candidates than urban women (Rokkan & Campbell, 1960; Rokkan & Valen, 1962).

Some research evidence questions the generalization that rural people are less likely to be active in politics than urban people. A community study in Oregon found no urban-rural differences in general community participation (their index included nonpolitical activities) (Agger & Ostrom, 1956). In Sweden, farmers were more active in voting than persons employed in many other industries, but they were not as active as employers (Karlsson, 1958a). Slightly higher voting turnout rates were found for rural Indiana counties than for urban counties (Robinson & Standing, 1960). Rural voting is also high in France and Italy.

In Japan, the general urban-rural differences described above do not hold. Several studies in Japan since World War II show political participation, especially voting turnout, to be higher in the rural areas than in urban areas (Kyogoku & Ike, 1959; Masumi, 1961). Most of the reasons given for this finding suggest that urban persons are no closer to the center of Japanese society than rural persons. If anything, the tendency is in the other direction. Most urban areas, especially Tokyo, have grown very fast in recent years, and a large proportion of city dwellers are poorly integrated into their community. Rural areas show higher community integration; the houses are close together (not isolated, as farmhouses are in the United States); exposure to the mass media is generally higher in rural areas; and rural communities compete with one another in seeing who can produce the greater turnout.

A very important factor is the social structure of rural Japan, which is still semi-feudal in basic respects. Old and large landowning families are closely knit by kinship and friendship ties. There is an authoritarian tradition for the people to follow the political lead of the head of the clan; voting is taken as a sign of loyalty. These rural political machines are stronger than urban machines and are the basic strength of the conservative party in Japan. Rural people place more emphasis on the reputation and personality of candidates, whereas city dwellers must rely more on party labels as a guide to voting.

City areas in Japan have experienced a much higher percentage of candidates offering themselves for public office. Many of these candidates have little reputation and status and meager city background. This seriously increases the information demands and costs for city voters. As the evolution toward urbanization proceeds, and as more adequate means are found to integrate the masses into urban life, one would expect the center of Japanese life to shift to the cities and the participation rates of urban and rural dwellers to follow more closely the pattern found in Western countries.

Size of community also relates to political participation. Generally, **the larger the community the higher the rate of participation.** Metropolitan areas have the highest participation rates, smaller cities and towns are next, and rural areas have the lowest rates (Campbell, et al., 1960; Campbell & Kahn, 1952; Connelly & Field, 1944; Gronseth, 1955; Korchin, 1946). A study in Sweden found higher rates in small towns and big cities, with medium-size cities somewhat less (Karlsson, 1958a). The Survey Research Center's 1956 election data show a .28 tau beta correlation between percentage of manufacturing employment in a county and the Campaign Activity Index; most counties with a high percentage of manufacturing are metropolitan counties.

MEMBERSHIP AND ACTIVITY IN GROUPS

The point was made in Chapter I (p. 17), and supported by many studies, that general group activity is highly related to participation in politics. This close relationship occurs not only because many of the same personal and social characteristics lead to both political and nonpolitical participation, but also because groups are important mobilizers of political action by their members. Organizations facilitate turnout, recruit candidates, and boost party membership (Hartenstein & Liepelt, 1962; Lane, 1959; Lipset, 1960b; McClosky & Dahlgren, 1959; Rokkan, 1962a). This holds, of course, only for organizations that desire to mobilize their membership politically; some organizations may have a norm favoring political apathy (Rosenberg, 1954-1955).

It is possible to speak of persons belonging to groupings even though there is no formal organization which they have joined. For example, it is common in politics to speak of ethnic minorities as groups, even though the accident of birth is the only criterion for membership. Despite their loose structure, these groupings have a discernible impact on political behavior, especially on the direction of the vote. Political commentators often try to predict how the "Jewish vote" or the "Polish vote," for example, is going to go in a forthcoming election. Most important for our purposes is the point made earlier that *persons living in communities that are relatively homogeneous with respect to these groupings tend to have a somewhat higher rate of political participation.* Living in such a homogeneous environment seems to increase a sense of political effectiveness, facilitates communication about politics, strengthens participatory norms, and deepens group identification.[8]

Organizational mobilization, however, is especially important for relatively deprived groupings such as Negroes, low-status persons, and laboring persons to whom channels of influence and advancement by individual action may seem blocked. The recent spurt in growth and numbers of civil rights organizations for Negroes has enormously increased the participation of Negroes in politics. Several studies show that **labor union members are more likely to take an interest in politics, to have stronger stands on issues, and to vote**

[8] See Lane (1959, pp. 261-264) for an expanded discussion of these groupings and factors.

than are nonunion laboring persons (Campbell, et al., 1954; Campbell, et al., 1960; Campbell & Kahn, 1952; McPhee & Glaser, 1962; Tingsten, 1937). There are some exceptions: a study in Waukegan, Illinois, showed no difference in voting turnout between union and nonunion workers (M. Miller, 1952). A study of union locals in Columbus, Ohio, found significant differences in level of political activity from one union local to the next. Union members who had more information about their union, and who participated more in union affairs, were more likely to be active in politics ($r = .29$). The great majority of union members (these were CIO union locals) were agreed that participation by the union in politics was appropriate (Dawson, 1963). A study in Sweden reported that members of occupational groups were more likely to participate in politics (Karlsson, 1958a). Data from the 1956 election study conducted by the Survey Research Center show trends for persons who strongly identify with their groups or who believe in the legitimacy of group political action to be more likely to participate in politics; both correlations are of borderline significance, however.

Persons belonging to more than one group may find their groups pulling in different directions, or some groups may urge political action while others urge inaction. Such persons may be thought of as "cross-pressured." It has generally been found that persons in group cross-pressure are less likely to participate than those not cross-pressured (Benny, et al., 1956; Fuchs, 1955; Lipset, 1960b). Conversely, persons belonging to groups that are homogeneous in political direction are more likely to participate (McClosky & Dahlgren, 1959; McPhee & Glaser, 1962). The family is a highly homogeneous group with a very high rate of interaction; its influence on participation patterns as well as on voting choice is very high (Boynton & Bowman, 1964; Glaser, 1959; Kuroda, 1964; McPhee & Glaser, 1962; Marvick & Nixon, 1961; Wahlke, et al., 1962).

Education is an important variable stimulating participation in both nonpolitical and political groups (Agger & Goldrich, 1958; Allardt & Pesonen, 1960; Almond & Verba, 1963). Just as men are more likely than women to participate in politics, **men are more likely than women to be active in groups** (Allardt & Pesonen, 1960; Almond & Verba, 1963). *Communities with a high proportion of groups and institutions provide more opportunities for group participation and more readily integrate persons into community life* (Lipset, 1950).

COMMUNITY IDENTIFICATION

It was mentioned several times above that persons who are well integrated into their community tend to feel close to the center of community decisions and are more likely to participate in politics. One evidence of this is that **the longer a person resides in a given community, the greater the likelihood of his participation in politics** (Agger, et al., 1964; Allardt & Bruun, 1956; Birch, 1950; Birch & Campbell, 1950; Buchanan, 1956; Kitt & Gleicher, 1950; Lane, 1959; Lipset, 1960b; Tingsten, 1937). Although length of residence correlates with voting turnout, it seems especially relevant to gladiatorial activities. A newcomer to town very likely begins to vote after a year or so, but it usually takes some additional time before he is drawn into party work. Only after a few years of testing will community residents be inclined to entrust party office to a newcomer or encourage his candidacy for public office.

Another bit of evidence is that *homeowners are more likely to vote than renters* (M. Miller, 1952). A study of a Mississippi community found that persons who identified strongly with it were more likely to feel that their vote had political impact, and they were less likely to perceive their community as run by a small elite not subject to popular guidance (Buchanan, 1956). It is curious, yet understandable, that persons most estranged from politics and their community are most likely to perceive their community as run by a small clique of autocratic rulers. Additional evidence relative to community integration comes from data relating age to participation: *young people are not likely to become enmeshed in politics until they have become established in a job, a home, and start to raise a family* — but that is the topic of the next section.

LIFE CYCLE AND AGE

The point just made helps to explain the typical curve found when age is related to political participation. **Participation rises gradually with age, reaches its peak and levels off in the forties and fifties, and gradually declines above sixty** (Allardt & Bruun, 1956; Benny, et al., 1956; Campbell, et al., 1960; Campbell & Kahn, 1952; Jensen, 1960; Kuroda, 1964; Lipset, 1960b; Tingsten, 1937, reported supporting data from five countries). Other studies do not describe the curve but simply report that older persons are more likely to vote than younger (Berelson, et al., 1954; Birch & Campbell, 1950; Buchanan, 1956; Connelly & Field, 1944; Glaser, 1959; Korchin, 1946; Lazarsfeld, et al., 1944; McPhee & Glaser, 1962; M. Miller, 1952). A community study in Oregon found no relationship between age and turnout (Agger & Ostrom, 1956). In a recent study of four communities (two of which are in the South), it was found that young Negroes (under thirty-five) in the South were more active than older Negroes. Some of the active young Negroes were newcomers to their community, too, in contrast to the general finding for the four communities that newcomers are less likely to be active in politics (Agger, et al., 1964). Clearly, a dynamic emotional issue (civil rights) is at work here, creating an aberration on the normal pattern.

The variation with age is perhaps best explained by its relation to the life cycle. **The most apathetic group are the young unmarried citizens who are only marginally integrated into their community.**[9] **Several studies have found that married persons are more likely to participate in politics than single persons** (Allardt, 1956; Allardt & Bruun, 1956; Dogan & Narbonne, 1955; Glaser, 1959; Karlsson, 1958a; Lipset, 1960b; Norwegian election study tables; Tingsten, 1937). Other studies, however, found no relationship between marital status and political participation (Agger & Ostrom, 1956; M. Miller, 1952; Särlvik, 1961b). Possibly the relationship of marriage to participation is confounded by the fact that it is difficult for a couple with young children to find time

[9] Pesonen (1960) and data from the SRC's 1956 election study and the 1957 election study in Norway.

for politics. This factor is more important in determining gladiatorial participation than for voting. The Survey Research Center classifies its respondents by position in the life cycle (a combination of age, marital status, and age of children). A cross-tabulation of the CAI with life cycle shows the highest participation rates for married persons with no children or with older children.

The full array of data suggest, then, that there are three intervening variables relating age to participation: integration with the community, the availability of blocks of free time for politics, and good health. Integration with the community develops gradually with marriage, job responsibility, and acquiring a family; thus, participation rises gradually with advancing age, leveling off at about thirty-five or forty. Young children and other confinements delay the full opportunity for participation, especially for young mothers. Finally, in the twilight years, physical infirmities probably account for most of the decline in participation.

VARIATIONS BY SEX

The traditional division of labor which assigns the political role to men rather than women has not vanished. The finding that **men are more likely to participate in politics than women** is one of the most thoroughly substantiated in social science (Agger, et al., 1964; Allardt, 1956; Allardt & Pesonen, 1960; Almond & Verba, 1963; Benny, et al., 1956; Berelson, et al., 1954; Birch, 1950; Buchanan, 1956; Campbell & Cooper, 1956; Connelly & Field, 1944; Dogan & Narbonne, 1955; Gronseth, 1955; Grundy, 1950; Korchin, 1946; Kuroda, 1964; Lane, 1959; Lazarsfeld, et al., 1944; McPhee & Glaser, 1962; Pesonen, 1960; Pesonen, 1961; Rokkan, 1962b; Tingsten, 1937, data from five countries). Data supporting this proposition come from at least nine countries. The survey interviewer seeking respondents for a political study discovers after only a few house calls that there are significant remnants of the tradition in modern society. A favorite excuse for not wishing to be interviewed is to claim that the husband takes care of the family politics. The *Chicago Sun Times* on September 2, 1963, quoted a state representative from Arkansas about women meddling in politics: "We don't have that trouble up in Perry County. When our women get too nosey about something that doesn't concern them, we get another cow to milk or get them a little more garden to tend." Only a few years ago in Switzerland, a proposition to give women the right to vote failed of passage.

Economic and social modernization is slowly eroding this sex difference, however. The five-nation study found the differences in participation between the sexes least in the United States, followed by the United Kingdom, Germany, Mexico, and Italy; the difference was especially great in Italy (Almond & Verba, 1963, Ch. 13). Two community studies in the United States found no differences in participation by sex (Agger & Ostrom, 1956; M. Miller, 1952). Researchers in Finland found that when they controlled for marital status and age, the difference by sex disappeared (Allardt & Bruun, 1956). A comparative study between Norway and the United States found for both countries that the sex difference in participation was quite pronounced in lower SES areas, especially areas of primary economy, but that the sex difference almost disappeared in urban, upper-middle SES, well-educated strata. At the upper levels of politics (running for and holding party and public office) in both countries, men are more likely to participate than women, even if both sexes are high SES (Rokkan & Campbell, 1960). The Evanston survey found women significantly less likely than men to be party actives (Jensen, 1960). The Survey Research Center 1956 election data show men more likely than women to wear a button or to proselyte but not significantly more likely to give money, attend meetings, do campaign work, or join a political club.

The erosion of the sex difference in participation does not necessarily mean that women are becoming independent of men in choosing whom they will support; it means only that politics is less and less considered strictly a man's role. A good deal of solid evidence still suggests that wives follow their husband's lead in politics (sometimes vice versa), or at least that **husband and wife tend to support the same parties and candidates** (Campbell, et al., 1960; Glaser, 1959; Gronseth, 1955; Tingsten, 1937).

RELIGION

It is difficult to know if religion per se influences political behavior, because religious groupings tend to coincide with SES, ethnic, and racial groupings. It is virtually impossible to separate out religion from these other factors. In any case, religious differences in participation are slight. The general pattern found in the United States is that **Jews are slightly more active in politics than Catholics who, in turn, are slightly more active than Protestants** (Campbell & Kahn, 1952; Connelly & Field, 1944; Korchin, 1946). The Survey Research Center 1956 election data show Catholics more likely than Protestants to vote but not more likely to engage in gladiatorial activities; Jews were more likely to engage in both spectator and gladiatorial activities.

One can guess that factors of group cohesion and group tradition are important in differentiating the political behavior of religious groupings. It seems reasonable to suppose that Jews are the most cohesive of the groupings, Catholics next, and Protestants least cohesive, since that category is itself made up of many groups. Another factor might be that groups which fear religious discrimination and persecution participate more heavily in politics to forestall use of the machinery of the state for oppression. Groups without these fears would have less motive for political activity. No data could be found relevant to either of these hypotheses.

Studies relating political participation to specific Protestant denominations show a slight trend for Episcopalians and Presbyterians to be more active than the average Protestant; Baptists seemed to be a bit less active than the average (Jensen, 1960; Milbrath, 1956a). However, since the first two groupings have above-average SES and the last has below-average SES, the denominational difference may merely reflect an SES difference. A study in Waukegan, Illinois, found persons affiliated with a church more likely to vote than non-affiliates (M. Miller, 1952). The Survey Research Center 1956 election data show regular attenders at church more likely than average to vote but not more likely to engage in gladiatorial activities (it was reported in Chapter III that most people felt a duty to vote but few felt a duty to become a gladiator); nonattenders and nonaffiliates were less likely to participate in both spectator and gladiator activities. The reader is reminded of the relevance of this to the relationship between group participation and political participation previously discussed.

RACIAL AND ETHNIC MINORITIES

Physiological racial characteristics do not account for participation differences between races; rather, it is the relative social position of racial groupings that create these differences. It seems clear that in the United States, Negro and other racial minorities are located toward the periphery rather than toward the center of society. Generally, they have less education, fewer job opportunities, lower incomes, and fewer opportunities to interact with prominent people. It has repeatedly been found in nationwide studies in the United States that **Negroes participate in politics at a much lower rate than whites** (Campbell, et al., 1954; Campbell, et al., 1960; Woodward & Roper, 1950). In the Survey Research Center 1956 election data, this difference held not only for the Campaign Activity Index but also for all the specific acts included in the index. Whites were especially more likely to contribute money than Negroes (the racial difference is also an income difference) but were only slightly more likely to proselyte, attend meetings, and join political clubs.

The survey in Evanston (a relatively wealthy northern suburb of Chicago) found no significant difference in political participation between whites and Negroes (Jensen, 1960). The Evanston situation may be similar to that found in a study of New Haven, Connecticut, where Negroes were more likely than whites to participate in local politics. In New Haven, channels of political influence and advancement are open equally to Negroes and whites. Private channels of influence (e.g., connections and advancement in private business), however, are relatively much less accessible to Negroes. Politics, then, probably seems more enticing to the ambitious Negro than to the ambitious white (Dahl, 1961). Lane (1959) has suggested that ethnic minorities are more likely to participate in local politics than nonethnics.[10] The recent study of four communities found higher participation rates for Negroes than for whites in one of the southern communities (Agger, et al., 1964, p. 269). These scattered findings suggest that racial and ethnic minorities are not always on the periphery; in certain communities they may be at the center or have very good access to it. One must be cautious in generalizing about behavior from a mere racial or ethnic category.

An additional factor to center-periphery in explaining racial differences in participation is the pattern of discrimination against Negro participation in politics, particularly in the American South. Some of these factors were discussed in Chapter IV under legal restrictions on registration. In addition to legal restrictions working against Negro participation, there are social pressures such as ostracism and verbal abuse. Economic reprisals such as loss of a job or being evicted from rented quarters may be used to prevent voting and other political activity. Some pressures are unabashedly violent, such as beatings and killings.[11] Generally, *the higher the percentage of Negroes in an area, the greater the pressure to keep them from voting.* This generalization holds especially clearly in the rural South.

A current study of Negro participation in the South (not yet fully reported) turned up an interesting finding. Southern counties with a high rate of lynchings and with recent experience with violent racial conflict tended to have lower than average Negro registration. If, however, one or the other of these conditions was absent, the registration percentage was higher than if both were absent. Currently available data do not suggest an adequate interpretation for this pattern. The authors conclude that having a Negro organization to facilitate participation is a much more important factor determining registration than experience with violence. The presence of a white supremacy organization in counties with Negro organizations did not seem to affect Negro registration percentages

[10] See Lane (1959, Ch. 17) for a full exposition.

[11] For information on a variety of impediments to Negro voting in the South, see *Hearings* of the United States Commission on Civil Rights, New Orleans, Louisiana, 1960-1961 (Washington: U.S. Government Printing Office, 1961).

adversely. If, however, there was a white supremacy organization and no Negro organization in the county, the Negro registration was below average (Matthews & Prothro, 1963b).

Negro organizations have had marked success in mobilizing politically active people within an environment largely uncongenial to political participation. Some of these organizations have persuaded their followers to vote as a bloc. A study of Negroes in Florida politics found a significant amount of bloc voting (Price, 1955). In vigorously contested electoral contests between white candidates, a bloc of Negro votes can tip the balance toward candidates selected by Negro leaders. This gives important bargaining power to Negroes as they plead for policies helpful to their race. It is important in Negro bloc voting in the South that knowledge of the Negro-endorsed candidates be kept from the white community until the majority of the white ballots have been cast, otherwise the Negro endorsement may act as the "kiss of death" among white voters. The Negro bloc vote in Durham, North Carolina, managed in that fashion, has been a significant swing factor in many elections there.

If a minority is prevented from using normal political channels for the redress of grievances, does it turn to extraordinary means or even attempt to destroy the political system? Little research evidence could be found dealing with this question. Extreme alienation accompanied by feelings of futility and despair may lead to a withdrawal into isolation; this is the feeling of anomie discussed in Chapter III. Apparently, many American Negroes had this posture toward politics until very recently, and, conceivably, a majority do even today. Sometimes, however, a deprived minority begins to feel that its situation may be improved if some extraordinary means are used to tap the latent political power of the group. If such a feeling arises in a group, the psychological pain of the deprivation becomes all the more poignant.

Currently, dark-skinned peoples all around the world seem to be caught up in a "revolution of rising expectations." As their expectations rise, they can no longer be content with the slow processes of social and political change. American Negroes in recent years have turned to sit-ins, boycotts, and street demonstrations as their choice of extraordinary political means when ordinary means failed or were too slow. Some recent research by the author in the summer of 1963 showed most whites rejecting demonstrations as a viable means of political protest, but Negroes tending to embrace the tactic as legitimate and viable.

It is important that most of the Negro community has chosen to accept rather than try to overthrow the existing political system. Some minority-group members, however, may believe that action within the system is futile; at the same time they may feel that they must try something drastic to dislodge the equilibrium of the system. Such persons may try to subvert the system or sweep it away. We need to know more about the conditions under which persons who feel politically deprived shift to extraordinary or destructive means in order to redress their grievances.

So far in this book, we have concentrated on explaining the political participation patterns of individual human beings. While that in itself is an interesting intellectual challenge, political scientists eventually hope to explain the workings of the larger political system in which those individuals live. How does individual political behavior link up to and determine the behavior of the system? What kinds of system characteristics might we expect, knowing what we do about individual behavior? How much participation, by whom, and in what ways is healthy for democracy? Social science does not, as yet, have good answers to these questions. In the next chapter, we shall, however, take a closer look and bring what little knowledge and insight we do possess to bear upon them.

VI

POLITICAL PARTICIPATION AND CONSTITUTIONAL DEMOCRACY

MOST AMERICANS have been told, and have come to believe by the time they reach adulthood, that in order for democracy to flourish, it is essential for citizens to be interested in, informed about, and active in politics. If democracy is going to be rule "of the people, by the people, and for the people," the people, by definition, must be interested and active. Many citizens believe that a decision made by all the people is better than a decision made by only part of the people. When only part of the people participate, the government is likely to be directed so as to violate the interests of the nonparticipators. Disinterest and apathy are not approved because, should they become widespread, power could easily be usurped and the quality of government seriously decline. An important preventive is to have a societal norm proclaiming a duty for all citizens to be interested, informed, and active.

It should be obvious from reading the foregoing pages that very few United States citizens measure up to that prescription. Although the data are not quite so good for other countries, those we do have suggest that very few persons living in Western democracies measure up to it either. Is there reason, then, to fear for the future of democracy? This question has received a good deal of attention by some eminent political scientists in recent years. (Almond & Verba, 1963, Ch. 15; Berelson, 1952; Berelson, et al., 1954, Ch. 14; Campbell, et al., 1960, Ch. 20; Dahl, 1954; Dahl, 1961, Bk VI; Duncan & Lukes, 1963; Eckstein, 1961; Key, 1961, Ch. 21; Lane,

1959, Ch. 22; Lane, 1962; Lipset, 1960b, Ch. 13; McClosky, 1964; Prothro & Grigg, 1960). Although these scholars are not in total agreement in their analyses, none expresses great concern about the future of democracy. One reason for this lack of intense concern is that these scholars are confronted by evidence from many societies, accumulated over a considerable period of time, that, despite the low level of political interest and activity, democratic governments continue to flourish and provide reasonably satisfactory governance for their citizens.

In reconciling the fact of low participation with the fact of adequately functioning democracies, political scientists have enlarged their understanding of the political process and of the role of the average citizen in that process. The role of the citizen has evolved into something different from that envisaged by classical democratic theorists such as John Locke. He had in mind a small homogeneous society where most persons were engaged in primary economic activities (agriculture, forestry, fishing, and the like) and where any average man was considered qualified to hold public office and to resolve public issues (which usually were much simpler than those confronting society today). Each man was expected to take an active role in public affairs.

Modern society, in contrast, has evolved a very high division of labor, not only in the economic sector but also in politics and government. Political roles have become highly differentiated and specialized. This enables some men (elected and appointed officials) to devote their full attention to the complex public issues facing modern society. This division of labor allows other men (most of the citizens) to pay relatively little attention to public affairs. Politics and government are a peripheral rather than a central concern in the lives of most citizens in modern Western societies. As long as public officials perform their tasks well, most citizens seem content not to become involved in politics.

The fact of indifference to politics by many citizens should not be taken to mean that government would function well if citizens ignored it completely. In order to keep public actions responsive to the wishes and desires of the people, citizens must at least participate in the choice of their public officials. The institutions of modern democracies have so evolved that policy leadership is left in the hands of elected officials who at periodic intervals go before the people at an election to see which of two or more competing elites will have policy leadership in the next ensuing period. Both the leaders and the public acknowledge the essentiality of this electoral link between the public and its governing elite.

The burden upon the citizen is much less if he is called upon only to select who his rulers will be than if he is asked to decide the pros and cons of an abstract policy. Furthermore, choices of public officials confront the citizen only at periodic elections, thus taking very little of his time. Society has evolved helpful mechanisms, called political parties, to simplify further the choice between alternative sets of public officials. Instead of having to become informed about a number of individual candidates, the citizen can manage simply by knowing the record and reputation of the political parties under whose labels the candidates run. Parties also are helpful in calling the voter's attention to the failures of the opposition party and to their own successes. The citizen does not need to dig for information, it is literally thrust at him.

Another device for keeping public officials responsive to the people is to require and insure open channels of communication, so that citizens who so wish can be heard or consulted when public officials are making policy decisions. In part, this is achieved by constitutional provisions for freedom of speech, press, assembly, and petition. Society also has evolved social institutions, such as interest groups and the mass media, which keep citizens informed of what public officials are doing and public officials informed of what citizens want. The fact that top officials are placed there by election is very significant in insuring that channels of communication stay open between the public and their leaders. If an official should refuse to listen (thus closing the channel), he would probably pay for his folly by losing his position at the next election.

As we think about the role of the average citizen, then, we should not expect him to give a lot of attention to, and be active in resolving, issues of public policy. Nor should we expect him to stand up and be counted on every issue that comes along. The most we can expect is that he will participate in the choice of decision-makers and that he will ask to be heard if an issue comes along that greatly concerns him or on which he can make some special contribution. Many citizens do not even vote or speak up on issues, yet their passive role has the consequence of accepting things as they are. Indeed, it is impossible to escape at least a passive role in the choice of decision-makers. The choice process can proceed and government can continue to function even if many citizens choose to be so inactive as to fail to vote.

In evaluating citizen roles, we should keep in mind that citizens play two roles at once. At the same time that they try to make the government respond to their wishes, citizens also must play the role of obedient subjects of the regime under which they live. The participant and subject roles pull in opposite directions, and it is important that they be kept in balance. It is difficult for a compliant subject also to question the performance of his rulers and to try to influence their policy decisions. Similarly, it is difficult for a very active and intense participant in politics to subject himself readily to every policy and law decided on by the government. Most citizens work out a balance between the two roles in their daily lives, although there are individual differences in emphasis; some lean more toward the subject role, and others lean more toward the participant role. The moderately active, rather than the highly active person is more likely to achieve satisfaction in balancing the two roles.[1]

A similar type of balance needs to be achieved at the system level, too. We want a government that is responsive to the wishes of the people but, at the same time, we want an effective government that is able to carry policies through to completion. There is a high probability of conflict between these two objectives. A government overly responsive to every whim of the public cannot pursue a consistent policy. The Fourth French Republic, which saw twenty changes of government in the twelve years following World War II, is

[1] Much of this argument is indebted to Almond & Verba (1963).

a good example of a government made ineffective by responding too readily to every fluctuation in public opinion. Conversely, a government which pursued a given program without paying any attention to the wishes and desires of the public would be thought of as autocratic and unsatisfactory. Most dictatorships are in this latter category. In maintaining a balance between responsiveness and the power to act, the system is aided by the efforts of individual citizens to balance their participant and subject roles. As subjects, they tend to allow a government to develop and pursue a policy for a certain period before passing judgment. As participants, they scrutinize the actions of officials, communicate their policy desires to the officials, and prepare to replace them with other officials if they do not perform adequately. The system balance is further aided by the fact that some individuals prefer to emphasize the role of subject, while others prefer to emphasize the role of participant. If everyone were highly active in politics, or if everyone were passively obedient, it would be more difficult to maintain system balance between responsiveness and power to act.

Moderate levels of participation help societies find another type of balance, that between consensus and cleavage.[2] It is in the very nature of politics that disputes will arise concerning issues and candidates, thus producing cleavages in the society. These must be bridged in some manner, however, if the society is to cohere and function adequately. Agreement on some larger principle, even though it is vague and platitudinous, often helps to bridge a cleavage.[3] Resolution of a conflict by peaceful means, such as an election, facilitates movement toward consensus. The important point here is that societies having large numbers of people who are intensely interested and active in politics (it is virtually impossible to have high activity without intense interest) tend to have wide and deep cleavages that are very difficult to bridge. A current example is the controversy over civil rights in the

[2] Berelson (1952) and Almond & Verba (1963) have made this point.
[3] McClosky (1964) has argued that agreement on large abstract principles is functional for political society, even if there is little agreement on specific applications of those principles.

American South. The intense feelings on both sides of that issue have assuredly stimulated active participation in politics by many who were formerly apathetic, but their political activities have also served to deepen the cleavage between the contending forces, making consensus increasingly remote. It is much easier to forget about past disputes or to take a broad perspective on present ones if those disputes are not considered vital by the participants. It is paradoxical that the kind of issue that stimulates widespread participation in politics is also the kind of issue likely to create wide cleavages in society.

Although it must be conceded that governments continue to function adequately with moderate to low levels of participation in politics, would they function even better if many more people became highly active? Although it can be argued that participation in politics develops character,[4] there is doubt that the society as a whole would benefit if intense interest and active involvement in politics became widespread throughout the population.

We would expect to find, in a society where most adults are intensely interested and involved in politics, that political concerns have moved from the periphery to the center of life interests for most persons. Probably most social relationships, in such a society, would become politicized. Some of the new African one-party states, Ghana, for example, are characterized by high politicization of social relationships. In a highly politicized society, political considerations determine a person's opportunities for education, for a job, for advancement on the job, for a place to live, for goods to enjoy. Furthermore, politics determines the thoughts a citizen can express, the religion he follows, his chances for justice. Such a permeation of politics into all aspects of life is antithetical to the basic principle of limited government in a constitutional democracy. There is a consensus in limited constitutional democracies that all the relationships (areas of life) mentioned above are out of bounds to politics.

If societies could be arrayed along a continuum according

[4] Duncan & Lukes (1963) have cited this as a reason for holding to high participation as a democratic norm.

to the level of politicization of relationships, at the one extreme all social relationships in the society would be politicized; at the opposite extreme, none of them would be. It is difficult to imagine societies being on either extreme, but some examples come to mind that lean strongly toward extremes. Life in medieval Europe, with its fixed class divisions, hereditary rulers, and prescriptive norms for every aspect of social relationships, is an example of a society close to the nonpoliticized extreme. Some politics-like choices were made in the governing hierarchy of the Roman Catholic Church and also within the courts of princes and kings, but so many human relationships were prescribed by customs, norms, and rules that only a small area of life was left open to political choice-making.

Approaching the highly politicized extreme are several new one-party states in Africa and the one-party Communist states of eastern Europe. A few areas of life are not politicized in these societies, especially relationships governed by tradition, but even these are under assault by forces bent on sweeping away the old order and using political passions as a weapon. Limited constitutional democracies, on the other hand, tend to be only moderately politicized. Citizens in these societies expect politicization of some aspects of life, such as decisions about land, resources, goods, and services held in common. By mutual consent, however, other areas are outside politics. In the five-nation study, about 90 per cent of respondents in Great Britain and the United States said it would make no difference if their child married a supporter of the opposition party. They are "saying, in effect, that personal relationships ought to be governed by values other than political ones. The family ought not to be allowed to be divided by partisan considerations" (Almond & Verba, 1963, p. 297). Sometimes the boundaries between political and nonpolitical areas are spelled out in written constitutions (e.g., the freedom of speech and freedom of religion guarantees in the Bill of Rights); sometimes they are arrived at by common consent and tradition (e.g., parents have the primary right and responsibility in the bringing up of their children).

Knowing the boundaries of politics is basic to the ability

of citizens to discriminate legitimate from illegitimate actions by their rulers. Being able to discriminate legitimate from illegitimate actions is, in turn, basic to the ability of a body politic to act in concert to forestall tyrannous actions by their rulers. The social wisdom which enables a body politic to discriminate areas rightfully governed by politics from areas rightfully outside politics has evolved slowly and painfully over many centuries in Western society. Such boundaries would be difficult to maintain if a high percentage of citizens should become intensely interested and involved in politics. A study of participation rates and of the factors stimulating participation suggests that there is little likelihood that intense political interest and involvement will develop so long as government functions adequately, enabling citizens to keep politics as a peripheral concern in their lives.

The point that high levels of political interest and participation may not be beneficial to constitutional democracy should not be taken to mean that moderate levels of participation automatically guarantee the maintenance of constitutional democracy. A special burden of responsibility for the maintenance of the system rests on the shoulders of the political elites. If these elites are to perform their roles adequately, it is important that they array themselves into two or more competing groups (usually called political parties). As these elites compete for the support of the voters, they perform functions of vigil and criticism *vis-à-vis* their opponents that moderately interested and active citizens might not perform for themselves. Partisan criticism functions best if it is tempered by the realization that after the next election the elite currently in the role of critic may be called upon to govern. This tempered criticism not only gives the party in power a chance to carry a program through to completion and stand responsible for it, but it also enables bridging of cleavages and helps maintain over-all coherence of the society.

Several conditions are critical to the adequate functioning of a system of competitive elites in a constitutional democracy.[5] It is important that the elites be committed to democratic values and believe in the rules of the game. It must be

[5]This section is largely indebted to Key (1961, Ch. 21).

taken for granted, for example, that the elites will compete for mass support and that expression of that support in an election will determine which elite will rule for the ensuing period. Several bits of research suggest that participation in politics builds a commitment to democratic values and that elites are much more likely to understand and adhere to specific applications of general democratic principles than are average citizens (Almond & Verba, 1963; McClosky, 1964; Prothro & Grigg, 1960). An elite in power must have a live-and-let-live policy *vis-à-vis* its opponents out of power; elite political actors should be gladiators but not revolutionaries. Property rights may be important to insure that opponents out of power have some way to support themselves until they can regain power. From another perspective, no elite will readily relinquish power, should it be defeated in an election, if it has no alternative base of economic support. That base might be income-earning property, practice of a profession, jobs in industry not controlled by the government, and so forth. An elite also will be reluctant to relinquish power if it is convinced that its opponents will destroy the group, perhaps by imprisonment or other harassment, once the opponents have been given power.

In order that the interests of all sectors of society be adequately taken care of by the government, it is important that each elite recruit from many sectors of society. An elite from a single class or group would have difficulty gaining the confidence of the people, and competitive elites would be reluctant to entrust it with the reins of power. New recruits should have easy access to the center of power in the elite to prevent the inner group from getting out of touch with the people. It is vital that the recruits be socialized to elite norms and customs, especially basic democratic principles and the rules of the political game.

The system demands much less from the political beliefs and behavior of the mass of the citizens than from the elites. To perform its role, the attentive public must believe in the right of the public to watch and to criticize the behavior of the elites. It also needs a minimal sense of involvement in public matters and a sense of loyalty to the whole community rather than to only a segment of the society. It must perform the minimal chore of selecting among the elites at election time. This low level of attention and control by the mass of the public leaves a wide latitude to the elected elite for creative leadership.

Although we expect only this minimal surveillance by the public and their participation in the choice of elites, is even this effort too much to expect? What is to prevent a society from becoming widely apathetic and allowing an unscrupulous elite to destroy the chances for an opposing group to compete fairly? In the final analysis, there is no iron-clad guarantee that this will not happen; eternal vigilance is still the price of liberty. Careful training of elite members in the norms and rules of democratic politics is one insurance against such an eventuality. Another is the outcry from the opposing group against the tactics of the party in power. This outcry has meaning, however, only if the public is listening, understands, and responds decisively.

In order for the public to respond adequately to dangers to their political system, it is essential that the system be kept open. There are two aspects to this openness. First, the communications network which provides the major linkage between actors in the political system must be kept open. Further, this network should carry a fairly high level of political content so that actors can, with minimum effort, find out what is going on in politics and government at any time. Lack of an open communications network would make it easier for an unscrupulous elite to subvert democracy. Almost the first act of elites seizing power by *coup d'état* is to grasp control of the communications system.

Secondly, the system should be kept open so that any citizen who so chooses can readily become active in politics at any time. Conversely, gladiators should be able to retire from politics readily and gracefully whenever they choose. This is important not only in circulating and replenishing elite memberships but also to the proper role behavior of gladiators, spectators, and apathetics. The potentiality that apathetics may become spectators and that spectators may become gladiators is an important property of the system confining and controlling the behavior of political elites.

> A good deal of citizen influence over governmental elites may entail no activity or even conscious intent of citizens. On the contrary, elites may anticipate possible demands and activities and act in response to what they anticipate. They act responsively, not because citizens are actively making demands, but in order to keep them from becoming active (Almond & Verba, 1963, p. 487).

In this respect, it is important to continue moral admonishment for citizens to become active in politics, not because we want or expect great masses of them to become active, but rather because the admonishment helps keep the system open and sustains a belief in the right of all to participate, which is an important norm governing the behavior of political elites.

> The democratic myth of citizen competence... has significant consequences. For one thing, it is not pure myth: the belief in the influence potential of the average man has some truth to it and does indicate real behavioral potential. And whether true or not, the myth is believed (Almond & Verba, 1963, p. 487).

It is a curious social fact that a norm, such as that which says citizens should be interested and active in politics, which is violated wholesale, still can be an important ingredient in the functioning of the political system. Should that norm wither or vanish, it would be much easier for unscrupulous elites to seize power and tyrannize ordinary citizens. Elites believing in that norm are more likely to welcome new recruits, are more likely to relinquish office easily when defeated in an election, are more likely to try to inform and educate their followers, are more likely to keep communication channels open and listen to the desires of the people, than are elites not believing in that norm. Perhaps one of the reasons the norm remains viable is that elites realize a decline of the norm could spell their own doom as they compete for the power to govern.

SUMMARY

Recapitulation of the foregoing argument, in brief form, may help the reader to see where it is leading. (1) Most citizens in any political society do not live up to the classical democratic prescription to be interested in, informed about, and active in politics. (2) Yet, democratic governments and societies continue to function adequately. (3) It is a fact that high participation is not required for successful democracy. (4) However, to insure responsiveness of officials, it is essential that a sizable percentage of citizens participate in choosing their public officials. (5) Maintaining open channels of communication in the society also helps to insure responsiveness of officials to public demands. (6) Moderate levels of participation by the mass of citizens help to balance citizen roles as participants and as obedient subjects. (7) Moderate levels of participation also help balance political systems which must be both responsive and powerful enough to act. (8) Furthermore, moderate participation levels are helpful in maintaining a balance between consensus and cleavage in society. (9) High participation levels would actually be detrimental to society if they tended to politicize a large percentage of social relationships. (10) Constitutional democracy is most likely to flourish if only a moderate proportion of social relationships (areas of life) are governed by political considerations. (11) Moderate or low participation levels by the general public place a special burden or responsibility on political elites for the successful functioning of constitutional democracy. (12) Elites must adhere to democratic norms and rules of the game and have a live-and-let-live attitude toward their opponents. (13) A society with widespread apathy could easily be dominated by an unscrupulous elite; only continuous vigilance by at least a few concerned citizens can prevent tyranny. (14) Elite recruitment and training is an especially important function. (15) To help insure final control of the political system by the public, it is essential to maintain an open communications system, to keep gladiator ranks open to make it easy for citizens to become active should they so choose, to continue moral admonishment for citizens to become active, and to keep alive the democratic myth of citizen competence.

It would be difficult to prove the validity of the above argument with research findings. For lack of evidence, many of the asserted relationships must remain hypothetical for the time being. Certain norms or preferred states for society have had to be posited (e.g., that governments should be both responsive and effective); others might disagree with those preferences. The points were put forward with the hope that they will stimulate discussion leading all of us to a clearer understanding of the dynamics of democracy. If this analysis is correct, present levels and patterns of participation in politics do not constitute a threat to democracy; they seem, in fact, to be a realistic adjustment to the nature of modern society. The political processes of that democracy may not be close to the ideal of the classical theorists, but they may well be the best possible approximation to popular control of government that can be achieved in modern, industrialized, mobile, mass society.

APPENDIX ON
SCALES AND INDEXES

ANOMIE SCALE DEVELOPED BY JOHN SCHAAR

Schaar selected the following two items from the "efficacy scale": "People like me don't have any say about what the government does." "Sometimes politics and government seems so complicated that a person like me can't really understand what's going on." In addition, the following two items were taken from the "personal effectiveness scale": "I have often had the feeling that it's no use to try to get anywhere in this life." "There's not much use for me to plan ahead because there's usually something that makes me change my plans." Agreement with each of the items was coded as anomic. The items were scaled by Guttman techniques, and respondents could fall in any of five positions (0, 1, 2, 3, 4) on the scale. Since all the items are scored in the same direction, the scale is subject to response-set bias; therefore, care was taken to apply a statistical control for response set when analyzing the relationship of the scale to other variables.

CAMPAIGN ACTIVITY INDEX

Respondents in the 1956 election study were asked whether they had voted and also the following questions:

"I have a list of some of the things that people do that help a party or a candidate win an election. I wonder if you could tell whether you did any of these things during the last election campaign." ____

"Did you talk to any people and try to show them why they should vote for one of the parties or candidates?"

"Did you give any money or buy tickets or anything to help the campaign for one of the parties or candidates?"

"Did you go to any political meetings, rallies, dinners, or things like that?"

"Did you do any other work for one of the parties or candidates?"

"Do you belong to any political club or organization?"

"Did you wear a campaign button or put a campaign sticker on your car?"

Nonvoters were given a score of zero and are generally spoken of in this book as apathetics. Voters who had not participated in any other way received a score of 1. Voters who had talked to someone else or had worn a button or put a sticker on their car were given a score of 2. Persons with scores of 1 or 2 are classified as spectators in this book. Persons who had voted and performed any one of the other four acts (give money, attend a meeting, do work, join a club) were given a score of 3. If they had done two or more of the four acts, they were given a score of 4. Persons scoring 3 or 4 are called gladiators in this book.

SENSE OF CITIZEN DUTY

Respondents were asked to agree or disagree with the following four statements:

"It isn't so important to vote when you know your party doesn't have a chance to win."

"A good many local elections aren't important enough to bother with."

"So many other people vote in the national election that it doesn't matter much to me whether I vote or not."

"If a person doesn't care how an election comes out, he shouldn't vote in it."

Persons disagreeing with those statements were scored as having a sense of duty. Respondents fell in one of five positions (0, 1, 2, 3, 4) on the scale. For a detailed discussion of the scale, see Campbell, et al. (1954, pp. 194-199).

SENSE OF POLITICAL EFFICACY

A measure of variations in the strength of the sense of political efficacy among respondents was constructed from expressions of agreement or disagreement with the following statements.

"I don't think public officials care much what people like me think."

"Voting is the only way people like me can have any say about how the government runs things."

"People like me don't have any say about what the government does."

"Sometimes politics and government seems so complicated that a person like me can't really understand what's going on."

Disagreement with the items was treated as efficacious response. The items were interspersed in the schedule with other statements included for other purposes. The responses were grouped into five types. Variations in the sense of political efficacy, so measured, had a positive relationship with variations in political participation. For a detailed discussion of the concept of the sense of political efficacy, see Campbell, et al. (1954, pp. 187-194).

INDEX OF ISSUE FAMILIARITY

Respondents were asked if they had an opinion on the following sixteen issues:

"The government ought to cut taxes even if it means putting off some important things that need to be done."

"The government in Washington ought to see to it that everybody who wants to work can find a job."

"This country would be better off if we just stayed home and did not concern ourselves with problems in other parts of the world."

"The government ought to help people get doctors and hospital care at low cost."

"The United States should give economic help to the poorer countries of the world even if they can't pay for it."

"If Negroes are not getting fair treatment in jobs and housing, the government in Washington should see to it that they do."

"The government ought to see to it that big business corporations don't have much say about how the government is run."

"The best way for this country to deal with Russia and Communist China is to act just as tough as they do."

"If cities and towns around the country need help to build more schools, the government in Washington ought to give them the money they need."

"The United States should keep soldiers overseas where they can help countries that are against communism."

"The government should leave things like electric power and housing for private businessmen to handle."

"The government ought to see to it that labor unions don't have much to say about how the government is run."

"The United States should be willing to go more than half-way in being friendly with the other countries of the world."

"The government ought to fire any government worker who is accused of being a communist even though they can't prove it."

"The United States should give help to foreign countries even if they are not as much against communism as we are."

"The government in Washington should stay out of the question of whether white and colored children go to the same school."

For each issue on which the respondent had an opinion, he was also asked, "Is the government going too far, doing less that it should, or doing just about right?" If a person had an opinion on the issue and also had a judgment on what the government was doing, he was regarded as "familiar" with the issue. The number of issues with which a person was familiar was then summed to compose the index.

PERSONAL EFFECTIVENESS SCALE

Although four positively scored and four negatively scored items were included in the schedule of questions, only the four negatively scored items were included in the scale for which data are reported in Table III.3. They were:

"I would rather decide things when they come up than always try to plan ahead."

"I seem to be the kind of person that has more bad luck than good luck."

"There's not much use for me to plan ahead because there's usually something that makes me change my plans."

"I have often had the feeling that it's no use to try to get anywhere in this life."

Persons disagreeing with those items were scored as effective. Care was taken to apply a statistical control for response-set bias when analyzing the relationship of the scale to other variables.

PSYCHOLOGICAL INVOLVEMENT

The measure of psychological involvement is in form a measure of concern about the particular presidential campaign but probably also taps a more general psychological concern about politics. It rests on responses to two questions. Respondents were asked in the early warm-up phase of the pre-election interview: "Generally speaking, would you say that you personally care a great deal which party wins the presidential election this fall or that you don't care very much which party wins?" Replies to this question were coded on a five-point scale from least to most "care" about the election outcome. Another question was: "Some people don't pay much attention to the political campaigns. How about you, would you say that you have been very much interested, somewhat interested, or not much interested in following the political campaigns so far this year?" By combination of the responses to these two questions, individuals were ranked on an index of psychological involvement.

BIBLIOGRAPHY

Abrams, Mark
1957-   "Press, Poll and Votes in Britain since the 1955 General
1958   Elections," *Public Opinion Quarterly*, XXI (Winter), 543-
         547.
Adorno, Theodore W., Else Frenkel-Brunswik, Daniel J. Levinson,
    and R. N. Sanford
1950   *The Authoritarian Personality*. New York: Harper.
Adrian, Charles R.
1952   "Some General Characteristics of Nonpartisan Elections,"
         American Political Science Review, XLVI (September),
         766-776.
Agger, Robert E.
1956a   "Lawyers in Politics," *Temple Law Quarterly*, XXIX (Sum-
         mer), 434-452.
1956b   "Power Attributions in the Local Community," *Social
         Forces*, XXXIV (May), 322-331.
Agger, Robert E., and Daniel Goldrich
1958   "Community Power Structures and Partisanship," *Amer-
         ican Sociological Review*, XXIII (August), 383-392.
Agger, Robert E., Daniel Goldrich, and Bert E. Swanson
1964   *The Rulers and the Ruled: Political Power and Impotence
         in American Communities*. New York: Wiley.
Agger, Robert E., Marshall Goldstein, and Stanley Pearl
1961   "Political Cynicism: Measurement and Meaning," *The
         Journal of Politics*, XXIII (August), 477-506.
Agger, Robert E., and Vincent Ostrom
1956   "Political Participation in a Small Community," in Heinz
         Eulau, Samuel J. Eldersveld, and Morris Janowitz, eds.,

Political Behavior. Glencoe, Ill.: The Free Press. Pp. 138-148.

Alexander, Franz
1959   "Emotional Factors in Voting Behavior," in Eugene Burdick and Arthur J. Brodbeck, eds., American Voting Behavior. Glencoe, Ill.: The Free Press. Pp. 300-307.
Allardt, Erik
1956   Social Struktur oc Politisk Activitet. Helsinki: Soderstroms.
1962   "Community Activity, Leisure Use and Social Structure," Acta Sociologica, VI (fasc. 1-2), 67-82.
Allardt, Erik, and Kettil Bruun
1956   "Characteristics of the Finnish Non-voter," Transactions of the Westermarck Society, III, 55-76.
Allardt, Erik, Pentti Jartti, Faina Jyrkilä, and Vrjö Littunen
1958   "On the Cumulative Nature of Leisure Activities," Acta Sociologica, III (fasc. 4), 165-172.
Allardt, Erik, and Pertti Pesonen
1960   "Citizen Participation in Political Life in Finland," International Social Science Journal, XII, No. 1, 27-39.
1965   "Structural and Non-structural Cleavages in Finnish Politics," in Seymour M. Lipset and Stein Rokkan, eds., Party Systems and Voter Alignments. Vol. IV of the International Yearbook of Political Behavior Research. New York: The Free Press of Glencoe.
Allport, Gordon W.
1929   "The Composition of Political Attitudes," American Journal of Sociology, XXXV (September), 220-238.
1945   "The Psychology of Participation," Psychological Review, LII (May), 117-132.
Almond, Gabriel
1954   The Appeals of Communism. Princeton: Princeton University Press.
Almond, Gabriel, and Sidney Verba
1963   The Civic Culture. Princeton: Princeton University Press.
Anderson, H. Dewey
1935   "The Educational and Occupational Attainment of Our National Rulers," Scientific Monthly, XL (June), 511-518.
Barkley, David W.
1962   "The Political Conservatism of Older People," paper pre-

pared for the annual meetings of the American Political Science Association, Washington, D. C., September.

Benny, Mark, and Phyllis Geiss
1950   "Social Class and Politics in Greenwich," *British Journal of Sociology,* I (December), 310-327.

Benny, Mark, A. P. Gray, and R. H. Pear
1956   *How People Vote: A Study of Electoral Behavior in Greenwich.* London: Routledge and Kegan Paul.

Berdahl, Clarence
1942   "Party Membership in the United States, I and II," *American Political Science Review,* XXXVI, 16-50, 241-262.

Berelson, Bernard R.
1949   "Communications and Public Opinion," in Wilbur Schramm, ed., *Mass Communications.* Urbana: University of Illinois Press. Pp. 496-512.
1952   "Democratic Theory and Public Opinion," *Public Opinion Quarterly,* XVI (Fall), 313-330.

Berelson, Bernard R., Paul F. Lazarsfeld, and William N. McPhee
1954   *Voting.* Chicago: University of Chicago Press.

Berelson, Bernard R., and Gary A. Steiner
1964   *Human Behavior: An Inventory of Scientific Findings.* New York: Harcourt, Brace & World.

Birch, A. H.
1950   "The Habit of Voting," *Journal of the Manchester School of Economic and Social Studies,* XVIII (January), 75-82.
1959   *Small-Town Politics: A Study of Political Life in Glossop.* London: Oxford University Press.
1960   "England and Wales," in *Citizen Participation in Political Life,* issue of *International Social Science Journal,* XII, No. 1, 15-26.

Birch, A. H., and Peter Campbell
1950   "Voting Behavior in a Lancashire Constituency," *British Journal of Sociology,* I (September), 197-208.

Bone, Hugh, and Austin Ranney
1963   *Politics and Voters.* New York: McGraw-Hill.

Bonham, John
1952   "The Middle Class Elector," *British Journal of Sociology,* III (September), 222-230.
1954   *The Middle Class Vote.* London: Faber & Faber.

Boskoff, Alvin, and Harmon Zeigler
1964   *Voting Patterns in a Local Election*. Philadelphia: Lippincott.

Boynton, George Robert, and Lewis Bowman
1964   The Recruitment of Political Activists: A Case Study. Unpublished manuscript.

Browning, Rufus P., and Herbert Jacob
1964   "Power Motivation and the Political Personality," *Public Opinion Quarterly*, XXVIII (Spring), 75-90.

Buchanan, William
1956   "An Inquiry into Purposive Voting," *The Journal of Politics*, XVIII (May), 281-296. Also in Bobbs-Merrill Reprint Series, No. PS-34.

Buck, Philip W.
1963   *Amateurs and Professionals in British Politics*. Chicago: University of Chicago Press.

Burdick, Eugene, and Arthur J. Brodbeck, eds.
1959   *American Voting Behavior*. Glencoe, Ill.: The Free Press.

Butler, David E.
1952   *The British General Election of 1951*. London: Macmillan.
1955   *The British General Election of 1955*. London: Macmillan.
1959   *Elections Abroad*. London: Macmillan.

Butler, David E., and Richard Rose
1960   *The British General Election of 1959*. London: Macmillan.

Campbell, Angus
1960   "Surge and Decline: A Study of Electoral Change," *Public Opinion Quarterly*, XXIV (Fall), 397-418.
1962   "The Passive Citizen," *Acta Sociologica*, VI (fasc. 1-2), 9-21.

Campbell, Angus, Phillip Converse, Warren Miller, and Donald Stokes
1960   *The American Voter*. New York: Wiley.

Campbell, Angus, and Homer C. Cooper
1956   *Group Differences in Attitudes and Votes*. Ann Arbor: University of Michigan, Institute for Social Research, Survey Research Center.

Campbell, Angus, Gerald Gurin, and Warren Miller.
1953   "Political Issues and the Vote: November, 1952," *American Political Science Review*, XLVII (June), 359-385.

1954   *The Voter Decides.* Evanston, Ill.: Row, Peterson.

Campbell, Angus, and Robert L. Kahn

1952   *The People Elect a President.* Ann Arbor: University of Michigan, Institute for Social Research, Survey Research Center.

Campbell, Angus, and Henry Valen

1961   "Party Identification in Norway and the United States," *Public Opinion Quarterly,* XXV (Winter), 505-525.

Campbell, Donald T., and Donald W Fiske

1959   "Convergent and Discriminant Validation by the Multi-trait-Multimethod Matrix," *Psychological Bulletin,* LVI (March), 81-105.

Campbell, Peter W., and A. H. Birch

1950   "Politics in the North-West [of Britain]," *Journal of the Manchester School of Economic and Social Studies,* XVIII (September), 217-243.

Campbell, Peter W., D. Dennison, and Allen Potter

1952   "Voting Behavior in Droylsden in October, 1951," *Journal of the Manchester School of Economic and Social Studies,* XX (January), 57-65.

Christie, Richard, and Peggy Cook

1958   "A Guide to Published Literature Relating to the Authoritarian Personality Through 1956," *Journal of Psychology,* XLV (April), 171-199.

Christie, Richard, Joan Havel, and Bernard Seidenberg

1958   "Is the F Scale Irreversible?" *Journal of Abnormal and Social Psychology,* LVI (March), 143-159.

Clapp, Charles L.

1963   *The Congressman: His Work as He Sees It.* Washington: The Brookings Institution.

Connelly, Gordon M., and Harry H. Field

1944   "The Non-Voter: Who He Is, What He Thinks," *Public Opinion Quarterly,* VIII (Summer), 175-187

Constantini, Edmond

1963   "Intraparty Attitude Conflict: Democratic Party Leadership in California," *Western Political Quarterly,* XVI (December), 956-972.

Converse, Phillip E.

1958   "The Shifting Role of Class in Political Attitudes and Behavior," in Eleanor Maccoby, et al., eds., *Readings in Social Psychology*. New York: Holt, Rinehart and Winston. Pp. 388-399.

Converse, Phillip, and Georges Dupeux
1961   "Some Comparative Notes on French and American Political Behavior." UNESCO Seminar, Bergen, Norway, June. (Mimeographed.)
1962   "Politicization of the Electorate in France and the United States," *Public Opinion Quarterly*, XXVI (Spring), 1-24.

Coser, Rose Lamb
1951   "Political Involvement and Interpersonal Relations," *Psychiatry*, XIV (May), 213-222.

Cutright, Phillips
1963   "Measuring the Impact of Local Party Activity on the General Election Vote," *Public Opinion Quarterly*, XXVII (Fall), 372-386.

Cutright, Phillips, and Peter H. Rossi
1958   "Grass Roots Politicians and the Vote," *American Sociological Review*, XXIII (April), 171-179.

Dahl, Robert A.
1954   *A Preface to Democratic Theory*. Chicago: University of Chicago Press.
1961   *Who Governs? Democracy and Power in an American City*. New Have' Yale University Press.
1963   *Modern Poi.:ical Analysis*. Englewood Cliffs, N. J.: Prentice-Hall.

Davies, James
1954   "Charisma in the 1952 Campaign," *American Political Science Review*, XLVIII (December), 1083-1102.
1963   *Human Nature in Politics*. New York: Wiley.

Dawidowicz, Lucy, and Leon J. Goldstein
1963   *Politics in a Pluralist Democracy*. New York: Institute of Human Relations Press.

Dawson, Richard
1963   The Local Union and Political Behavior: Some Aspects of Group Influence on Individual Attitudes and Behavior. Unpublished doctoral dissertation, Northwestern University.

Dean, Dwight G.
1960   "Alienation and Political Apathy," *Social Forces,* XXXVIII (March), 185-189.

Dennis, Wayne
1930   "Registration and Voting in a Patriotic Organization," *Journal of Social Psychology,* I (May), 317-318.

Dogan, Mattei
1961   "Political Ascent in a Class Society: French Deputies 1870-1958," in Dwaine Marvick, ed., *Political Decision-Makers.* Glencoe, Ill.: The Free Press. Pp. 57-90.

Doggan, Mattei, and J. Narbonne
1955   *Les Francaises Face à la Politique.* Paris: Armand Colin.

Douvan, Elizabeth, and A. Walker
1956   "The Sense of Effectiveness in Public Affairs," *Psychological Monographs,* Vol. LXX, No. 22.

Duncan, Graeme, and Steven Lukes
1963   "The New Democracy," *Political Studies,* XI (June), 156-177.

Duverger, Maurice
1954   *Political Parties.* New York: Wiley.

Eckstein, Harry
1961   *A Theory of Stable Democracy.* Research Monograph No. 10. Princeton: Princeton University, Woodrow Wilson School of Public and International Affairs, Center of International Studies.

Eldersveld, Samuel J.
1956   "Experimental Propaganda Techniques and Voting Behavior," *American Political Science Review,* L (March), 154-165.

1964   *Political Parties: A Behavioral Analysis.* Chicago: Rand McNally.

Eldersveld, Samuel J., and Richard W. Dodge
1954   "Personal Contact or Mail Propaganda? An Experiment in Voting Turnout and Attitude Change," in Daniel Katz, et al., eds., *Public Opinion and Propaganda.* New York: Dryden. Pp. 532-542.

Epstein, Leon
1956   "British Mass Parties in Comparison with American Par-

ties," *Political Science Quarterly*, LXXI (March), 97-125.

Erbe, William
1964   "Social Involvement and Political Activity," *American Sociological Review*, XXIX (April), 198-215.

Eulau, Heinz
1962   *Class and Party in the Eisenhower Years*. New York: The Free Press of Glencoe.

Eulau, Heinz, William Buchanan, LeRoy C. Ferguson, and John C. Wahlke
1959   "Socialization of American State Legislators," *Midwest Journal of Political Science*, III (May), 188-206.

Eulau, Heinz, and Peter Schneider
1956   "Dimensions of Political Involvement," *Public Opinion Quarterly*, XX (Spring), 128-142.

Fensterwald, Bernard, Jr.
1958   "The Anatomy of American 'Isolationism' and Expansionism," *Journal of Conflict Resolution*, II (December), 280-309.

Fenton, John H., and Kenneth N. Vines
1957   "Negro Registration in Louisiana," *American Political Science Review*, LI (September), 704-713.

Festinger, Leon, Stanley Schachter, and Kurt Back
1950   *Social Pressures in Informal Groups*, New York: Harper.

Forthal, Sonya
1946   *Cogwheels of Democracy: A Study of a Precinct Captain*. New York: William-Frederick Press.

Foskett, J. M.
1955   "Social Structure and Social Participation," *American Sociological Review*, XX (August), 431-438.

Freeman, Howard· E., and Morris Showel
1951-   "Differential Political Influence of Voluntary Associations,"
1952   *Public Opinion Quarterly*, XV (Winter), 703-714.

Freeman, J. Leiper
1958   "Local Party Systems: Theoretical Considerations and a Case Analysis, *American Journal of Sociology*, LXIV (November), 282-289.

Frenkel-Brunswik, Else
1952   "The Interaction of Psychological and Sociological Factors in Political Behavior," *American Political Science Review*, XLVI (March), 44-65.

Fuchs, Lawrence H.
1955 "American Jews and the Presidential Vote," *American Political Science Review,* XLIX (June), 385-401.
1956 *The Political Behavior of American Jews.* Glencoe, Ill.: The Free Press.

Glantz, Oscar
1960 "The Negro Voter in Northern Industrial Cities," *Western Political Quarterly,* XIII (December), 999-1010.
1959 "Protestant and Catholic Voting Behavior in a Metropolitan Area," *Public Opinion Quarterly,* XXIII (Spring), 73-82.

Glaser, William A.
1958 "Intention and Voting Turnout," *American Political Science Review,* LII (December), 1030-1040.
1959 "The Family and Voting Turnout," *Public Opinion Quarterly,* XXIII (Winter), 563-570.

Goldhamer, Herbert
1950 "Public Opinion and Personality," *American Journal of Sociology,* LV (January), 346-354.

Goldman, Ralph
1956 "Move—Lose Your Vote," *National Municipal Review,* XLV (January), 6-10.

Gosnell, Harold F.
1927 *Getting Out the Vote.* Chicago: University of Chicago Press.
1930 *Why Europe Votes.* Chicago: University of Chicago Press.
1937 *Machine Politics.* Chicago: University of Chicago Press.
1948 *Democracy, the Threshold of Freedom.* New York: Ronald.

Gronseth, Erik
1955 *The Political Role of Women in Norway.* Oslo: Institute for Social Research. (Mimeographed.) Excerpts from a contribution to the Norwegian report to the UNESCO study of the political role of women. Oslo: Oslo University, Institute of Sociology, 1953. First published in Maurice Duverger, *The Political Role of Women.* Paris: UNESCO. Pp. 194-221.

Grundy, J.
1950 "Non-Voting in an Urban District," *Journal of the Manchester School of Economic and Social Studies,* XVIII (January), 83-99.

Guttman, Louis
1949 "The Basis for Scalogram Analysis," in Samuel Stouffer, et al., eds., *Measurement and Prediction.* Vol. IV of *Studies*

in Social Psychology in World War II. Princeton: Princeton University Press. Pp. 60-90. Also in Bobbs-Merrill Reprint Series No. S-413.

Guttsman, W. L.
1951 "The Changing Social Structure of the British Political Elite, 1886-1935," *British Journal of Sociology,* II (June), 122-134.
1960 "Social Stratification and Political Elite," *British Journal of Sociology,* XI (June), 137-150.

Hacker, Andrew, and Joel D. Aberbach
1962 "Businessmen in Politics," in *Symposium on the Electoral Process: Part I,* published as Spring, 1962, issue of *Law and Contemporary Problems.* Durham, N. C.: Duke University School of Law. Pp. 260-279.

Harned, Louise
1957 Participation in Political Parties: A Study of Party Committeemen. Unpublished doctoral dissertation, Yale University.
1961 "Authoritarian Attitudes and Party Activity," *Public Opinion Quarterly,* XXV (Fall), 393-399.

Hartenstein, Wolfgang, and Klaus Liepelt
1961 *The Active Minority in Germany: Some Notes on Participation Data,* UNESCO Seminar, Bergen, Norway, June. (Mimeographed.)
1962 "Party Members and Party Voters in West Germany," *Acta Sociologica,* VI (fasc. 1-2), 43-52.

Hastings, Philip K.
1954 "The Non-Voter in 1952: A Study of Pittsfield, Massachusetts," *Journal of Psychology,* XXXVIII (October), 301-312.

Heard, Alexander
1960 *The Costs of Democracy.* Chapel Hill: University of North Carolina Press.

Hennessy, Bernard
1959 "Politicals and Apoliticals: Some Measurements of Personality Traits," *Midwest Journal of Political Science,* III (November), 336-355.

Himmelstrand, Ulf
1960a *Social Pressures, Attitudes, and Democratic Processes.* Stockholm, Sweden: Almqvist & Wiksell.

1960b "Verbal Attitudes and Behavior: A Paradigm for the Study of Message Transmission and Transformation," *Public Opinion Quarterly*, XXIV (Summer), 224-250.

Høyer, Svennik
1961 *Political Commitment and Audience Coverage: A Content Analysis of Norwegian Newspapers.* UNESCO Seminar, Bergen, Norway, June. (Mimeographed.)

Hull, Clark L.
1943 *Principles of Behavior.* New York: Appleton-Century-Crofts.

Huntington, Samuel P.
1950 "A Revised Theory of American Party Politics," *American Political Science Review*, XLIV (September), 669-677.

Jacob, Herbert
1962 "Initial Recruitment of Elected Officials in the U. S.: A Model," *The Journal of Politics*, XXIV (November), 703-716.

Janda, Kenneth
1965 "A Comparative Study of Political Alienation and Voting Behavior in Three Suburban Communities," in *Studies in History and the Social Sciences: Studies in Honor of John A. Kinneman.* Normal, Ill.: Illinois State University Press.

Janosik, Edward G.
1962 *Report on Political Activity of Philadelphia Businessmen.* Philadelphia: University of Pennsylvania, Wharton School of Finance and Commerce.

Janowitz, Morris, and Dwaine Marvick
1953 "Authoritarianism and Political Behavior," *Public Opinion Quarterly*, XVII (Summer), 185-201.
1956 *Competitive Pressure and Democratic Consent.* Michigan Governmental Studies No. 32. Ann Arbor: University of Michigan, Bureau of Public Administration. A summarization of this report appears in Heinz Eulau, et al., eds., *Political Behavior.* Glencoe, Ill.: The Free Press, 1956. Pp. 275-286.

Jennings, M. Kent
1964 *Community Influentials: The Elites of Atlanta.* New York: The Free Press of Glencoe.

Jensen, Jack
1960 Political Participation: A Survey in Evanston, Illinois. Unpublished master's thesis, Northwestern University.

Karlsson, Georg

1958a "Voting Participation among Male Swedish Youth," *Acta Sociologica*, III (fasc. 2-3), 98-111.

1958b "Political Attitudes among Male Swedish Youth," *Acta Sociologica*, III (fasc. 4), 220-241.

Katz, Daniel, and Samuel J. Eldersveld

1961 "The Impact of Local Party Activity upon the Electorate," *Public Opinion Quarterly*, XXV (Spring), 1-24.

Katz, Elihu

1957 "The Two-Step Flow of Communication: An Up-to-Date Report on an Hypothesis," *Public Opinion Quarterly*, XXI (Spring), 61-78.

Katz, Elihu, and Paul Lazarsfeld

1955 *Personal Influence*. Glencoe, Ill.: The Free Press.

Kessel, John H.

1964 Cognitive Dimensions and Political Activity. (Unpublished manuscript.)

Key, V. O., Jr.

1949 *Southern Politics in State and Nation*. New York: Alfred A. Knopf.

1954 "The Direct Primary and Party Structure," *American Political Science Review*, XLVIII (March), 1-26.

1955 "A Theory of Critical Elections," *The Journal of Politics*, XVII (February), 3-18.

1959 "Secular Realignment and the Party System," *The Journal of Politics*, XXI (May), 198-210.

1961 *Public Opinion and American Democracy*. New York: Alfred A. Knopf.

Key, V. O., Jr., and Frank Munger

1959 "Social Determinism and Electoral Decision: The Case of Indiana," in Eugene Burdick and Arthur J. Brodbeck, eds., *American Voting Behavior*. Glencoe, Ill.: The Free Press. Pp. 281-299.

Kilpatrick, Franklin P., Milton C. Cummings, Jr., and M. Kent Jennings

1963 *The Image of the Federal Service*. Washington: The Brookings Institution.

Kitt, Alice S., and David B. Gleicher

1950 "Determinants of Voting Behavior," *Public Opinion Quarterly*, XIV (Fall), 393-412.

Knupfer, Genevieve
1947   "Portrait of the Underdog," *Public Opinion Quarterly,* XI (Spring), 103-114.
Korchin, Sheldon J.
1946   Psychological Variables in the Behavior of Voters. Unpublished doctoral dissertation, Harvard University.
Kornhauser, Arthur
1950   "Public Opinion and Social Class," *American Journal of Sociology,* LV (January), 333-345.
Kornhauser, Arthur, Albert J. Mayer, and Harold Sheppard
1956   *When Labor Votes.* New York: University Books.
Kornhauser, William
1959   *The Politics of Mass Society.* Glencoe, Ill.: The Free Press.
Kuroda, Yasumasa
1962   Political Socialization: Personal Political Orientations of Law Students in Japan. Unpublished doctoral dissertation, University of Oregon.
1964   *Measurement, Correlates, and Significance of Political Participation at the Community Level.* (Mimeographed.)
Kyogoku, Jun-ichi
1961   "Political Behavior Studies in Contemporary Japan," paper prepared for the Fifth World Congress of the International Political Science Association, Paris, September.
Kyogoku, Jun-ichi, and Nobutaka Ike
1959   *Urban-Rural Differences in Voting Behavior in Postwar Japan.* Reprinted as No. 66 of the Stanford University Political Science Series for the Proceedings of the Department of Social Sciences, University of Tokyo.
Lane, Robert E.
1955   "Political Personality and Electoral Choice," *American Political Science Review,* XLIX (March), 173-190.
1959   *Political Life: Why People Get Involved in Politics.* Glencoe, Ill.: The Free Press.
1962   *Political Ideology: Why the American Common Man Believes What He Does.* New York: The Free Press of Glencoe.
Lang, Kurt, and Gladys E. Lang
1956   "The TV Personality in Politics: Some Considerations," *Public Opinion Quarterly,* XX (Spring), 103-112.
Lasswell, Harold
1930   *Psychopathology and Politics.* Chicago: University of Chi-

cago Press. Reprinted in *The Political Writings of Harold Lasswell*. Glencoe, Ill.: The Free Press, 1951. Pp. 1-282.

1954　"The Selective Effect of Personality on Political Participation," in Richard Christie and Marie Jahoda, eds., *Studies in the Scope and Method of "The Authoritarian Personality."* Glencoe, Ill.: The Free Press. Pp. 197-225.

Lazarsfeld, Paul F., Bernard Berelson, and Hazel Gaudet
1944　*The Peoples' Choice*. New York: Duell, Sloan, and Pearce.

Lazarsfeld, Paul, and Robert Merton
1948　"Mass Communication, Popular Taste, and Organized Social Action," in Lyman Bryson, ed., *The Communication of Ideas*. New York: Harper. Pp. 95-118.

Lenski, Gerhard
1956　"Social Participation and Status Crystallization," *American Sociological Review*, XXI (August), 458-464.

Levin, Murray B.
1960　*The Alienated Voter*. New York: Holt, Rinehart and Winston.

Levinson, Daniel
1957　"Authoritarian Personality and Foreign Policy," *Journal of Conflict Resolution*, I (March), 37-47.

Lippit, Gordon, and Drexel Sprecher
1960　"Factors Motivating Citizens to Become Active in Politics as Seen by Practical Politicians," *Journal of Social Issues*, XXVI, No. 1, 11-18.

Lipset, Seymour Martin
1950　*Agrarian Socialism*. Berkeley: University of California Press.
1960a　"Party Systems and the Representation of Social Groups," *European Journal of Sociology*, I, No. 1, 50-85.
1960b　*Political Man*. Garden City, N. Y.: Doubleday.

Lipset, Seymour Martin, Paul Lazarsfeld, Allen Barton, and Juan Linz
1954　"The Psychology of Voting: An Analysis of Political Behavior," in Gardner Lindzey, ed., *Handbook of Social Psychology*, II, Cambridge, Mass.: Addison-Wesley, 1124-1175.

Litt, Edgar
1963　"Political Cynicism and Political Futility," *The Journal of Politics*, XXV (May), 312-323.

McCallum, R. B., and Alison Readman
1947   *The British General Election of 1945.* London: Oxford University Press.

McClosky, Herbert
1958   "Conservatism and Personality," *American Political Science Review,* LII (March), 27-45. Reprinted in S. Sidney Ulmer, ed., *Introductory Readings in Political Behavior.* Chicago: Rand McNally, 1961. Pp. 33-44.
1964   "Consensus and Ideology in American Politics," *American Political Science Review,* LVIII (June), 361-382.

McClosky, Herbert, and Harold E. Dahlgren
1959   "Primary Group Influence on Party Loyalty," *American Political Science Review,* LIII (September), 757-776. Reprinted in S. Sidney Ulmer, *Introductory Readings in Political Behavior.* Chicago: Rand McNally, 1961. Pp. 221-237.

McClosky, Herbert, Paul J. Hoffmann, and Rosemary O'Hare
1960   "Issue Conflict and Consensus among Party Leaders and Followers," *American Political Science Review,* LIV (June), 406-427.

Maccoby, Herbert
1958   "The Differential Political Activity of Participants in a Voluntary Association," *American Sociological Review,* XXIII (October), 524-532.

McConaughy, John
1950   "Certain Personality Factors of State Legislators in South Carolina," *American Political Science Review,* XLIV (December), 897-903.

McDill, Edward L., and Jeanne C. Ridley
1962   "Status, Anomia, Political Alienation and Political Participation," *American Journal of Sociology,* LXVIII (September), 205-217.

MacKenzie, W. J. M., and K. Robinson, eds.
1960   *Five Elections in Africa.* London: Oxford University Press.

McPhee, William N., and William A. Glaser, eds.
1962   *Public Opinion and Congressional Elections.* New York: The Free Press of Glencoe.

Mann, Dean
1964   *Federal Political Executives.* Washington: The Brookings Institution.

Marvick, Dwaine
1962   "The Middlemen of Politics," paper prepared for the annual meetings of the American Political Science Association, Washington, September.

Marvick, Dwaine, and Charles Nixon
1961   "Recruitment Contrasts in Rival Campaign Groups," in Dwaine Marvick, ed., *Political Decision-Makers.* Glencoe, Ill.: The Free Press. Pp. 193-217.

Maslow, Abraham H.
1943   "A Theory of Human Motivation," *Psychological Review,* L (July), 370-396.

Masumi, Junnosuke
1961   "Japanese Voting Behavior: A Changing Nation and the Vote," paper prepared for the Fifth World Congress of the International Political Science Association, Paris, September.

Matthews, Donald R., and James W. Prothro
1962   "Southern Racial Attitudes: Conflict, Awareness, and Political Change," *Annals of the American Academy of Political and Social Science,* CCCXLIV (November), 108-121.

1963a   "Social and Economic Factors and Negro Voter Registration in the South," *American Political Science Review,* LVII (March), 24-44.

1963b   "Political Factors and Negro Voter Registration in the South," *American Political Science Review,* LVII (June), 355-367.

1964a   "Negro Voter Registration in the South," in Allen P. Sindler, ed., *Change in the Contemporary South.* Durham, N. C.: Duke University Press. Pp. 119-149.

1964b   "Southern Images of Political Parties: An Analysis of White and Negro Attitudes," *The Journal of Politics,* XXVI (February), 82-111.

Mayntz, Renate
1961   "Citizen Participation in Germany: Nature and Extent," paper prepared for the Fifth World Congress of the International Political Science Association, Paris, September.

Meier, Dorothy L.
1963   "Anomia, Life Chances, Perceived Achievement, and
        Modes of Adaptation," paper prepared for the annual meet-
        ings of the American Sociological Association, Los Angeles,
        August.
Meier, Dorothy L., and Wendell Bell
1959   "Anomia and Differential Access to the Achievement of
        Life Goals," American Sociological Review, XXIV (April),
        189-202.
Merriam, Charles F., and Harold F. Gosnell
1924   Non-Voting. Chicago: University of Chicago Press.
Michels, Robert
1949   Political Parties. Glencoe, Ill.: The Free Press.
Milbrath, Lester W.
1956a   The Motivations and Characteristics of Political Contrib-
        utors: North Carolina General Election, 1952. Unpublished
        doctoral dissertation, University of North Carolina.
1956b   "Personality and Political Participation," paper prepared
        for the annual meetings of the Southern Political Science
        Association, Gatlinburg, Tenn., November.
1960a   Measuring the Personalities of Lobbyists. (Mimeographed.)
1960b   "Predispositions toward Political Contention," Western
        Political Quarterly, XIII (March), 5-18.
1962   "Latent Origins of Liberalism: Conservatism and Party
        Identification: A Research Note," The Journal of Politics,
        XXIV (November), 679-688.
1963   The Washington Lobbyists. Chicago: Rand McNally.
1965   "Political Participation in the States," in Herbert Jacob
        and Kenneth Vines, eds., Comparative State Politics.
        Boston: Little Brown. Ch. 2.
Milbrath, Lester W., and Walter Klein
1962   "Personality Correlates of Political Participation," Acta
        Sociologica, VI (fasc. 1-2), 53-66.
Miller, Mungo
1952   "The Waukegan Study of Voter Turnout Prediction," Public
        Opinion Quarterly, XVI (Fall), 381-398.
Miller, Warren E.
1955-   "Presidential Coat-tails: A Study in Political Myth and
1956   Methodology," Public Opinion Quarterly, XIX (Winter),
        353-368.

1956   "One-Party Politics and the Voter," *American Political Science Review*, L (September), 707-725.

1958   "The Socio-Economic Analysis of Political Behavior," *Midwest Journal of Political Science*, II (August), 239-255.

Milne, R. S., and Mackenzie, H. C.

1954   *Straight Fight: A Study of Voting Behavior in the Constituency of Bristol North-East at the General Election, 1951.* London: Hansard Society.

1958   *Marginal Seat.* London: Hansard Society.

Mitchell, William C.

1958   "Occupational Role Strains: The American Elective Public Official," *Administrative Science Quarterly*, III (September), 210-228. Also in Bobbs-Merrill Reprint Series No. PS-210.

1959   "The Ambivalent Social Status of the American Politician," *Western Political Quarterly*, XII (September), 683-698. Also in Bobbs-Merrill Reprint Series No. PS-209.

Mussen, Paul, and Anne Wyszynski

1952   "Personality and Political Participation," *Human Relations*, V (February), 65-82.

Neuman, Dale A.

1964   Work, Leisure and Political Behavior. Unpublished doctoral dissertation, Northwestern University.

Nicholas, H. G.

1951   *The British General Election of 1950.* London: Macmillan.

Parsons, Talcott

1957   "Voting and the Equilibrium of the American Party System," in Eugene Burdick and Arthur J. Brodbeck, eds., *American Voting Behavior*. Glencoe, Ill.: The Free Press. Pp. 80-120.

Pesonen, Pertti

1960   "The Voting Behavior of Finnish Students," in *Democracy in Finland*. Helsinki: Finnish Political Science Association. Pp. 93-104.

1961   "Citizen Participation in Finnish Politics," paper prepared for the Fifth World Congress of the International Political Science Association, Paris, September.

President's Commission

1963   *Report on Registration and Voting Participation.* Washington: U. S. Government Printing Office.

Price, Hugh Douglas
1955   "The Negro and Florida Politics," *The Journal of Politics*, XVII (May), 198-220. Also in Bobbs-Merrill Reprint Series No. PS-233.
Prothro, James W., and Charles M. Grigg
1960   "Fundamental Principles of Democracy: Bases of Agreement and Disagreement," *Journal of Politics*, XXII (May), 276-294.
Rhodes, E. C.
1938a   "The Exercise of the Franchise in London," *Political Quarterly*, IX (January-March), 113-119.
1938b   "Voting at Municipal Elections," *Political Quarterly*, IX (April-June), 271-280.
Rhyne, Edward
1958   "Political Parties and Decision Making in Three Southern Counties," *American Political Science Review*, LII (December), 1091-1108.
Riesman, David
1950   *The Lonely Crowd*. New Haven: Yale University Press.
1952   *Faces in the Crowd*. New Haven: Yale University Press.
Riesman, David, and Nathan Glazer
1950   "Criteria for Political Apathy," in Alvin Gouldner, ed., *Studies in Leadership*. New York: Harper. Pp. 540-547. Also in Bobbs-Merrill Reprint Series No. S-236.
Robinson, James A., and William H. Standing
1960   "Some Correlates of Voter Participation: The Case of Indiana," *The Journal of Politics*, XXII (February), 96-111.
Robinson, W. S.
1952   "The Motivational Structure of Political Participation," *American Sociological Review*, XVII (April), 151-156.
Rokeach, Milton
1960   *The Open and Closed Mind*. New York: Basic Books.
Rokkan, Stein
1955   "Party Preferences and Opinion Patterns in Western Europe: A Comparative Analysis," *International Social Science Bulletin*, VII, No. 4, 575-596.
1959   "Electoral Activity, Party Membership, and Organizational Influence," *Acta Sociologica*, IV (fasc. 1), 25-37.
1961   "Mass Suffrage, Secret Voting and Political Participation," *European Journal of Sociology*, II, No. 1, 132-152.

1962a   "Approaches to the Study of Political Participation," Introduction to special issue, edited by Rokkan, of *Acta Sociologica*, VI (fasc. 1-2), 1-8.

1962b   "The Comparative Study of Political Participation: Notes toward a Perspective on Current Research," in Austin Ranney, ed., *Essays on the Behavioral Study of Politics*. Urbana: University of Illinois Press. Pp. 47-90.

Rokkan, Stein, and Angus Campbell
1960   "Norway and the United States of America," in *Citizen Participation in Political Life*, issue of *International Social Science Journal*, XII, No. 1, 69-99.

Rokkan, Stein, and Henry Valen
1960   "Parties, Elections, and Political Behavior in the Northern Countries," a Review of Recent Research in O. Stammer, ed., *Politische Forschung*. Köln-Opladen: Westdeutscher Verlag. Pp. 120-125, bibliography at 237-249.

1962   "The Mobilization of the Periphery: Data on Turnout, Party Membership and Candidate Recruitment in Norway," *Acta Sociologica*, VI (fasc. 1-2), 111-158.

Rose, Arnold M.
1962   "Alienation and Participation: A Comparison of Group Leaders and the 'Mass,'" *American Sociological Review*, XXVII (December), 834-838.

Rosenberg, Morris
1951   "The Meaning of Politics in Mass Society," *Public Opinion Quarterly*, XV (Spring), 5-15.

1954-   "Some Determinants of Political Apathy," *Public Opinion*
1955   *Quarterly*, XVIII (Winter), 349-366.

1956   "Misanthropy and Political Ideology," *American Sociological Review*, XXI (December), 690-695.

1962   "Self-Esteem and Concern with Public Affairs," *Public Opinion Quarterly*, XXVI (Summer), 201-211.

Rosenzweig, Robert M.
1957   "The Politician and the Career in Politics," *Midwest Journal of Political Science*, I (May), 163-172.

Rossi, Peter H., and Phillips Cutright
1961   "The Impact of Party Organization in an Industrial Setting," in Morris Janowitz, ed., *Community Political Systems*. Glencoe, Ill.: The Free Press. Pp. 81-116.

Saenger, Gerhart H.
1945   "Social Status and Political Behavior," *American Journal of Sociology*, LI (September), 103-113. Also in Bobbs-Merrill Reprint Series No. 245.

Sanford, Fillmore
1950   *Authoritarianism and Leadership*. Philadelphia: Institute for Research in Human Relations.

Särlvik, Bo
1961a   "The Role of Party Identification in Voters' Perception of Political Issues," paper prepared for the Fifth World Congress of the International Political Science Association, Paris, September.
1961b   "The Swedish General Election of 1960." UNESCO Seminar, Bergen, Norway, June. (Mimeographed.)

Scheuch, Erwin K.
1961   "Leisure Patterns and Social Integration," paper prepared for UNESCO Seminar, Bergen, Norway, June. (Mimeographed.)

Schlesinger, Joseph A.
1957   "Lawyers and American Politics: A Clarified View," *Midwest Journal of Political Science*, I (May), 26-39.

Scott, William
1960   "International Ideology and Interpersonal Ideology," *Public Opinion Quarterly*, XXIV (Fall), 419-435.

Seligman, Lester G.
1961   "Political Recruitment and Party Structure," *American Political Science Review*, LV (March), 77-86.

Shils, Edward
1961   "The Intellectuals in Indian Political Development," in Dwaine Marvick, ed., *Political Decision Makers*. Glencoe, Ill.: The Free Press. Pp. 29-56.

Sigel, Roberta S.
1962   "Presidential Leadership Images, with Some Reflections on the Political Outlook of Negro Voters," paper prepared for the annual meetings of the American Political Science Association, Washington, September.

Sindler, Allan
1955   "Bi-Factional Rivalry as an Alternative to Two-Party Com-

petition in Louisiana," *American Political Science Review,* XLIX (September), 641-663.

Skinner, Burrhus F.
1953   *Science and Human Behavior.* New York: Macmillan.

Smith, M. Brewster, Jerome S. Bruner, and Robert W. White
1956   *Opinions and Personality.* New York: Wiley.

Smith, T. E.
1960   *Elections in Developing Countries.* New York: St. Martin's Press.

Srole, Leo
1951   "Social Dysfunction, Personality and Social Distance Attitudes," paper prepared for the annual meetings of the American Sociological Society, Chicago.

1956   "Social Integration and Certain Corollaries: An Exploratory Study," *American Sociological Review,* XXI (December), 709-716.

Standing, William H., and James A. Robinson
1958   "Inter-party Competition and Primary Contesting: The Case of Indiana," *American Political Science Review,* LII (December), 1066-1077.

Stokes, Donald
1962   "Popular Evaluations of Government: An Empirical Assessment," in Harlan Cleveland and Harold Lasswell, eds., *Ethics and Bigness.* New York: Harper.

Stokes, Donald, Angus Campbell, and Warren Miller
1958   "Components of Electoral Decision," *American Political Science Review,* LII (June), 367-387.

Suchman, Edward A., and Herbert Menzel
1955   "The Interplay of Demographic and Psychological Variables in the Analysis of Voting Surveys," in Paul Lazarsfeld and Morris Rosenberg, eds., *The Language of Social Research.* Glencoe, Ill.: The Free Press. Pp. 148-155.

Sussman, Leila
1959   "Mass Political Letter Writing in America: The Growth of an Institution," *Public Opinion Quarterly,* XIII (Summer), 203-212.

Thompson, Wayne E., and John E. Horton
1960   "Political Alienation as a Force in Political Action," *Social Forces,* XXXVIII (March), 190-195.

Tingsten, Herbert
1937   *Political Behavior: Studies in Election Statistics.* London: P. S. King.
1955   "Stability and Vitality in Swedish Democracy," *Political Quarterly*, XXVI (April-June), 140-151.
Valen, Henry
1961   "The Motivation and Recruitment of Political Personnel," paper prepared for UNESCO Seminar, Bergen, Norway, June. (Mimeographed.)
Wahlke, John C., Heinz Eulau, William Buchanan, and LeRoy C. Ferguson
1962   *The Legislative System: Explorations in Legislative Behavior.* New York: Wiley.
Warner, W. Lloyd, Paul P. Van Riper, Norman H. Martin, and Orvis F. Collins
1963   *The American Federal Executive: A Study of the Social and Personal Characteristics of the Civilian and Military Leaders of the United States Federal Government.* New Haven: Yale University Press.
Williams, Oliver P., and Charles R. Adrian
1959   "The Insulation of Local Politics under the Non-Partisan Ballot," *American Political Science Review*, LIII (December), 1052-1063.
Wolfinger, Raymond E.
1963   "The Influence of Precinct Work on Voting Behavior," *Public Opinion Quarterly*, XXVII (Fall), 387-398.
Woodward, Julian L., and Elmo Roper
1950   "Political Activity of American Citizens," *American Political Science Review*, XLIV (December), 872-885.
Wright, Charles R., and Herbert Hyman
1958   "Voluntary Association Memberships of American Adults: Evidence from National Sample Surveys," *American Sociological Review*, XXII (June), 284-294.
Yates, W. Ross
1962a   "The Function of Residence Requirements for Voting," *Western Political Quarterly*, XV (September), 469-488.
1962b   "Residence Requirements for Voting: Ten Years of Change," paper prepared for the annual meetings of the American Political Science Association, Washington, September.

Zeller, Belle, and Hugh A. Bone
1948   "The Repeal of P. R. in New York City—Ten Years in Retrospect," *American Political Science Review*, XLII (December), 1127-1148.
Ziff, Ruth
1948   The Effect of the Last Three Weeks of a Presidential Campaign on the Electorate. Unpublished master's thesis, Columbia University.

INDEX

Aberbach, J. D., 127
Abilities, personal, 44, 64
Accelerator effect, 41
Accuracy of political knowledge, 64
Achievement motive and participation, 82
Action: duration of, 6; extremity of, 6; intensity of, 6; expressive, 12; instrumental, 12; classification of dimensions of, 14; discrimination of legitimacy of, 148-149
Action, political. *See* Political action
Active-inactive dimension, 9
Active-passive dimension, 14
Actives, party, 26, 49
Activity, dimensions of, 9
Activity, gladiatorial, 57, 60, 61, 62, 106: and personal contact, 100; and closeness of vote, 103; and life cycle, 105; and status mobility, 117; and education, 123; and occupation, 126; and length of residence, 133; and religion, 137
Activity, nonpolitical community, 17
Activity, party. *See* Party activity
Activity, political: hierarchy of costs of, 19; level of, 41
Activity, spectator, 57, 60, 61, 66, 106: and personal contact, 100; and status mobility, 117; and occupation, 126
Adorno, T. W., 83n, 84
Affect toward politics, and competence, 77
Affection, 30
Age, 53: and efficacy, 58; and political sophistication, 68; and cynicism, 81; and participation, 134-135
Agger, R. E., 17n, 60, 64, 79, 80, 81, 96, 112, 113, 116, 120, 122, 124, 129, 132, 133, 134, 135, 136
Albany, N. Y., 65
Alienation, 78: defined, 79; and participation, 79; and environment, 80; in Italy, 80; and involvement

in social organization, 81; and SES, 81; and racial minorities, 140
Allardt, E., 17n, 39, 44, 45, 59, 79, 96, 103, 104, 108, 116, 119, 122, 124, 132, 133, 134, 135, 136
Almond, G., 3, 9n, 17, 22n, 39, 43, 45, 54, 56, 57, 58, 61, 63, 64, 72, 75, 76, 79, 80, 90, 91, 122, 123, 132, 133, 135, 136, 142, 145n, 146n, 150, 152
Anderson, H. D., 124, 126
Anomie, 78: defined, 78; and participation, 78, 79; and education, 79; and racial minorities, 140
Anomie scale, 78: operationalization of, 155
Anxiety, 55: and participation, 79
Apathetics, 20, 21, 52, 54, 55: and complexity of politics, 65
Attachment to party, 39
Attitudes, 30, 31, 36, 38, 48, 50: defined, 32; political, 50; intensity of, 50; positive, toward politics, 56; and behavior, 72; citizen-duty, and political efficacy, 63; foreign-policy, and political sophistication, 67
Attraction to politics, 55: intensity of, 52
Authoritarianism, 83: defined, 84; measured, 84; and efficacy, 85; and lobbyists, 85; and participation, 85, 86; and probability of voting, 85

Behavior, 38, 48: defined as continuous, 29; attitudes and, 72; beliefs and, 72; distance of personality from, 72; personality and, 73; influence of situation and personality on, 73. *See also* Political behavior
Beliefs, 30, 31, 35, 36, 38, 48, 50: community, 8; defined, 32; citizen-duty, 41; and political participation, 64; and behavior, 72

185

PRINTED IN U.S.A.